Verdi's Operas

Verdi's Operas

AN ILLUSTRATED SURVEY OF PLOTS, CHARACTERS, SOURCES, AND CRITICISM

EDITED BY
GIORGIO BAGNOLI

AMADEUS
PRESS

AN IMPRINT OF
HAL LEONARD CORPORATION

Edited by Giorgio Bagnoli, with texts by:
Mario Bortolotto
Claudio Casini
Adriano Cavicchi
Duilio Courir
Fedele D'Amico
Renato Di Benedetto
Gioacchino Lanza Tomasi
Mario Messinis
Leonardo Pinzauti

Amadeus Press
An Imprint of Hal Leonard Corporation
7777 West Bluemound Road
Milwaukee, WI 53213

Trade Book Division Editorial Offices
33 Plymouth St., Montclair, NJ 07042

Published in 2001 and 2013 as *Le Opere di Verdi:
Trame, Personaggi, Fonti, Critica, Fortuna,
Immagini* by Mondadori Electa S.p.A., Milan

English-language edition published in 2014 by
Amadeus Press

Printed in Italy

English-language translation by Jay Hyams
English-language typesetting by Michael Shaw

Library of Congress Cataloging-in-Publication
Data is available upon request.
Amadeus ISBN: 978-1-57467-448-4

www.amadeuspress.com

Note to the Reader

This book is among the many editorial projects inspired by the bicentennial of Verdi's birth. It is meant primarily as an introduction to his operas, but along the way it also provides background information on the history of the operas as well as insight into Verdi's personal life.

The book opens with a chronology of his life that provides historical background helpful to understanding his world. This is followed by all of Verdi's operas, arranged in chronological order, from *Oberto* (1839) to *Falstaff* (1893).

The chapter for each opera presents a complete and detailed overview of the plot with the order of events and highlighted important moments, followed by a history of the opera, how it came to be written, how it was received, and its place within Verdi's world. Also covered are the time and place of each opera's premiere and the first performers.

Many of Verdi's operas enjoy enduring fame, and the most famous—*Ernani, Rigoletto, Il Trovatore, La Traviata, Un Ballo in Maschera, La Forza del Destino, Don Carlos, Aida, Otello,* and *Falstaff*—are given special attention here by way of outstanding commentary selected from the *Guide to the Opera* (*Guida all'Opera*), published by Mondadori and, sadly, no longer in print. These citations from illustrious Italian musicologists and opera historians analyze important aspects of the operas, offering the reader further insight and depth.

Contents

Preface

Giuseppe Verdi and Richard Wagner were born the same year, 1813, and went on to dominate the world of European theatrical music during the second half of the 19th century. Verdi was born into the poverty of a peasant family and throughout his life remained tied to his origins, including the land of Parma. His was a simple and open spirit, but he was subject to profound existential crises; gifted with great humanity, Verdi was—from the human point of view, in terms of his character—profoundly different from Wagner, who was entirely caught up in his own superior status as an artistic genius.

The result is that the operas of Verdi are composed of an energy inspired by the common people joined to a unique characteristic of Italian music, the generosity of its melodic soul. Verdi's operas exist on the highest plane of the theatrical world with a felicitous dramatic expression that makes them an authentic popular art in the highest sense of the term. Without sidestepping the weak spots in his abundant production, or seeking to negate certain not infrequent moments of naïveté, I have approached Verdi as a man and musical composer of great immediacy and spontaneity; I have sought to cast light on the reasons behind his extraordinarily brilliant career, the upward sweep of which resulted from his genius for melodrama, from Oberto to Falstaff. In doing so I have sought to present and explain the greatness that animates his scores.

Verdi the man is always present beside Verdi the composer, a man who was a creation of Romanticism, with both its dark pessimisms and its bursts of passion. But Verdi was also sensitive to the social movements around him and had first-person experience of the long, tormented years leading up to the unification of Italy. Preserved intact in Verdi's operas are both the climate of warmth and the human ardor of that period of time.

Without descending into abstract musicological analyses or investigating any dark and scandalous aspects of his life, I have sought to provide an introduction to the true Verdi and by way of these pages make it possible for those who still don't know him to experience some of the creative power that made him an enduring point of reference in the history of music.

Giorgio Bagnoli

BIRTH CERTIFICATE OF GIUSEPPE VERDI

In the year 1813, on the 12th of October, at nine o'clock, before us as vice-mayor of the town council of Busseto, marriage official in the town council of the above, in the Taro Department, appeared Verdi Carlo, aged 28, innkeeper, living in Roncole; he presented to us a male child born on the 10th of the current month at eight in the morning, declared by himself and by his wife, Luigia Uttini, spinner, living in Roncole, and to whom he declared to give the names of Giuseppe, Fortunino, Francesco. These declarations were made in the presence of Romanelli Antonio, 51 years of age, doorkeeper of the town council, and of Carità Giacinto, 60 years of age, porter, living in Busseto.

After reading the following act to the declarants and to the witnesses, they have signed their names along with mine:

Verdi Carlo – Antonio Romanelli – Giacinto Carità – Vice-mayor Vitali

Giuseppe Verdi in a famous portrait by Giovanni Boldini from 1886 (opposite) and in a photograph from the last years of his life (inset).

CHRONOLOGY OF VERDI'S LIFE

1813 ● Born at Roncole near Busseto on October 10.

1820–1831 ● First studies at Roncole and Busseto; frequents the home of Antonio Barezzi.

1832–1835 ● With financial support from Busseto's Monte di Pietà and from Barezzi, he studies privately in Milan under Maestro Vincenzo Lavigna.

1836 ● Wins the competition to be music master of the town of Busseto. Marries Margherita Barezzi on May 4. Their two children, Virginia and Icilio, will die in infancy.

1839 ● The premiere at Milan's Teatro alla Scala of his opera *Oberto, Conte di San Bonifacio* on November 17 meets with considerable success.

1840 ● Sudden death of Margherita, on June 18. *Un Giorno di Regno* is performed at La Scala on September 5 and judged a fiasco.

1842 ● Triumph of *Nabucco* at La Scala on March 9. The female lead is Giuseppina Strepponi, already known to Verdi during the period of *Oberto*.

1843 ● *I Lombardi alla Prima Crociata* goes into performance at La Scala on February 11.

1844 ● *Ernani* premieres at the Teatro La Fenice in Venice on March 9. *I Due Foscari* opens at the Teatro Argentina in Rome on November 3.

1845 ● *Giovanna d'Arco* premieres at La Scala on February 15; *Alzira* opens at the Teatro San Carlo in Naples on August 12.

1846 ● *Attila* opens at the Teatro La Fenice in Venice on March 17.

1847 ● *Macbeth* opens at the Teatro della Pergola in Florence on March 14; *I Masnadieri* opens on July 22 in London, where Verdi meets Giuseppe Mazzini, an exiled proponent of Italian unification. *Jérusalem* (a reworking of *I Lombardi*) opens in Paris at the Opéra on November 26. Verdi begins living with Giuseppina Strepponi.

1848 ● Verdi is in Milan immediately after the Cinque Giornate (Five Days) uprising;

he buys the estate of Sant'Agata in Busseto. *Il Corsaro* opens at the Teatro Grande in Trieste on October 25.

1849 ● Verdi is in Rome during the Roman Republic; *La Battaglia di Legnano* premieres at the Teatro Argentina on January 27, *Luisa Miller* at the San Carlo in Naples on December 8.

1850 ● *Stiffelio* opens in Trieste on November 16.

1851 ● *Rigoletto* opens at La Fenice on March 11. Not long afterward, Verdi goes to Sant'Agata with Strepponi. On June 28 his mother, Luigia Uttini, dies.

1853 ● *Il Trovatore* opens at the Teatro Apollo in Rome on January 19. *La Traviata* premieres at La Fenice on March 6 and is judged a fiasco; it is redeemed, after some revisions, by a triumph the next year, again in Venice, at the Teatro San Benedetto.

1855 ● *Les Vêpres Siciliennes* opens at the Opéra in Paris on June 13.

1857 ● *Simon Boccanegra* premieres at La Fenice on March 12. *Aroldo* (a reworking of *Stiffelio*) opens at the Teatro Nuovo in Rimini on August 16.

1858 ● Verdi marries Giuseppina Strepponi on August 29 at Collonges-sous-Salève in Savoy. He is in Turin in September as an elected representative of the Parma provinces to offer them to Victor Emmanuel II for annexation to Piedmont.

1859 ● *Un Ballo in Maschera* opens at the Teatro Apollo in Rome on February 17.

1861 ● Elected deputy to the first Italian parliament, he is in Turin for the proclamation of the kingdom of Italy.

1862 ● On May 24, Verdi is in London for the premiere of the *Inno delle Nazioni* ("Anthem of the Nations"), with text by Arrigo Boito. He is in St. Petersburg for the premiere of *La Forza del Destino* on November 10 at the Imperial Theater.

1865 ● The reworked version of *Macbeth* opens April 21 in Paris at the Théâtre Lyrique.

1867 • Verdi's father dies at Busseto on January 14 while Verdi is in Paris, where *Don Carlos* premieres at the Opéra on March 11. In May he begins taking care of his cousin Maria Filomena Verdi, destined to become his sole heir. On July 21 Antonio Barezzi dies.

1868 • On June 30 Verdi visits Alessandro Manzoni in Milan. On November 13 Rossini dies; in his honor Verdi promotes a Requiem Mass to be written by sev-

eral Italian composers and for which he himself writes the "Libera me Domine."

1869 • The new version of *La Forza del Destino* opens at La Scala on February 27.

1871 • Premiere of *Aida* in Cairo on December 24.

1874 • Verdi conducts the *Messa da Requiem* he wrote for Manzoni in the Church of San Marco in Milan on May 22. He is named to the senate by Victor Emmanuel II.

1881 • *Simon Boccanegra*, largely reworked, is performed at La Scala on March 24.

1884 • Premiere of *Don Carlo* in the Italian version with four acts at La Scala on January 10.

1887 • *Otello* opens at La Scala on February 5.

1888 • The hospital at Villanova sull'Arda, paid for and maintained by Verdi, opens on November 6.

1889 • Verdi buys land in Milan for construction of the Casa di Riposo per Musicisti (Rest Home for Musicians).

1893 • *Falstaff* premieres at La Scala on February 9.

1897 • On November 14 Giuseppina Strepponi dies at Sant'Agata.

1898 • Verdi's choral *Stabat Mater, Laudi alla Vergine Maria*, and *Te Deum* are premiered at the Paris Opéra on April 7. They are performed together with his *Ave Maria* in the first complete performance of *Quattro Pezzi Sacri* (*Four Sacred Pieces*) in Vienna on November 13.

1901 • On January 27 Verdi dies in the Hotel de Milan in Milan. A simple funeral is held on January 30 for burial in the Cimitero Monumentale, and on February 26 a solemn funeral is held for the transportation of his body and that of Giuseppina Strepponi to the chapel of the Casa di Riposo per Musicisti.

Oberto, Conte di San Bonifacio

Dramma in two acts to a libretto by
Antonio Piazza and Temistocle Solera

FIRST PERFORMANCE
TEATRO ALLA SCALA, MILAN, NOVEMBER 17, 1839

FIRST PERFORMERS
ANTONIETTA MARINI-RAINIERI (LEONORA), MARY SHAW (CUNIZA),
MARIETTA SACCHI (IMELDA), LORENZO SALVI (RICCARDO),
IGNAZIO MARINI (OBERTO)

CHARACTERS

Cuniza, sister of Ezzelino da Romano (*mezzo-soprano*)
Riccardo, count of Salinguerra (*tenor*)
Oberto, count of San Bonifacio (*bass*)
Leonora, his daughter (*soprano*)
Imelda, Cuniza's confidante (*mezzo-soprano*)

CHORUSES AND EXTRAS
Lords, ladies, vassals, knights

TIME: 1228.
PLACE: In and around Ezzelino's palace in Bassano, northern Italy.

Oberto, Conte di San Bonifacio, title page of the libretto for the first performance, Milan, Ricordi, 1839.

PLOT

Background Events

After being defeated by Ezzelino da Romano, Oberto, count of San Bonifacio, was forced to cede his holdings to the rulers of Salinguerra and to take refuge in Mantua, leaving his daughter Leonora, orphaned of her mother, with a sister in Verona. There, Leonora was seduced and abandoned by a young man who was presented to her under a false name. The seducer is none other than Riccardo, count of Salinguerra, who is now infatuated with Ezzelino's sister, Cuniza. The story begins as Riccardo and Cuniza are about to celebrate their wedding.

OBERTO
CONTE DI S. BONIFACIO
DRAMMA IN DUE ATTI
DA RAPPRESENTARSI
NELL' I. R. TEATRO ALLA SCALA
L' AUTUNNO 1839.

Milano
PER GASPARE TRUFFI
M.DCCC.XXXIX

encourage her. Leonora and Oberto manage to get into the palace, find Cuniza, and inform her of Riccardo's betrayal of Leonora. Indignant, Cuniza summons the traitor, who, undone by the presence of Leonora and Oberto, is unable to find a plausible justification for his actions, thus proving his guilt.

Act II

Cuniza, wounded in her love, refuses to listen to Riccardo and wants instead to have him marry Leonora. This proposal conflicts with Oberto's desire for revenge, and after challenging Riccardo to a duel, he impatiently awaits the time for the duel. Just as the two challengers are about to cross swords, Leonora and Cuniza arrive. The two women have quite different feelings: Leonora thinks she still loves Riccardo, while Cuniza reprimands him once again, imposing the marriage on him as a means of repairing the harm done. Riccardo agrees to this solution and so, it seems, does the old count. "Seems," because not long afterward Riccardo, provoked by the fearless count, mortally wounds him and flees, full of remorse. Leonora finds her dying father and is brought, half-conscious, to Cuniza, who tries in vain to comfort her. A messenger arrives bearing the news that Riccardo is traveling toward distant lands; he is also ready to offer Leonora his hand and all his possessions. Leonora, however, does not listen to these words: her only desire is to end her days in prayer in a convent.

Left: Ezzelino da Romano (1194–1259), lord of Bassano and ruler of Vicenza, Verona, and Padua, was defeated and wounded in a battle at Cassano d'Adda. He was taken prisoner to Soncino, where he died.

Below: The young Verdi in a period photograph.

Act I

Knights, ladies, and vassals festively welcome the arrival of Riccardo on the eve of his marriage to Cuniza. Leonora arrives secretly, more determined than ever to get revenge for the outrage she has suffered. Oberto, too, at the risk of his life, arrives near the palace, resolved to punish his daughter and her seducer. Father and daughter meet and, after a dramatic encounter, find themselves united in their determination to seek revenge.

Meanwhile, in a room of the palace, Cuniza, far from taking joy in her coming marriage, is full of sorrowful forebodings; Riccardo vainly tries to

Right: A scene from *Oberto, Conte di San Bonifacio*, Teatro Regio, Parma, 1977–78 season.

Below: Miniature from the Manesse Codex depicting a medieval knight and his young squire.

BACKGROUND AND ANALYSIS

Verdi arrived in Milan in February 1839, bearing an opera he'd been working on for several years, as indicated by a series of letters he wrote between 1835 and 1839 to Pietro Massini, singing master and performance director of the Società Filarmonica of Milan. In one of these letters Verdi noted, "I'm writing the opera . . . Let me know about all the singers you've heard at the academy." Verdi was clearly thinking of having this opera, then called *Rocester*, presented at the Teatro dei Filodrammatici, the performance headquarters of the Società Filarmonica. The failure of this plan led to an attempt to have

it performed in Parma. In another letter to Massini, dated September 21, 1837, Verdi wrote, "It will not be difficult to have the opera *Rocester* performed during the carnival period in Parma." But this attempt, too, ended in failure.

Such was the situation until 1839, when the opportunity to finally have the opera performed seemed to again present itself. By then all traces of *Rocester*, based on a libretto by Antonio Piazza, had disappeared, and we learn from another letter that Verdi was working on the score for an opera. From this it can be deduced that he was reworking, with the help of the librettist Temistocle Solera, the score that was to later become *Oberto, Conte di San Bonifacio* (*Oberto, Count of San Bonifacio*). The relationship between *Rocester* and *Oberto* has never been clearly established, but beyond the question of how events unfolded, *Oberto* was performed on November 17 of that same 1839, receiving an excellent welcome from the public and critics, a success that earned Verdi

the commission for three new operas to be performed in the same theater.

The course of Verdi's career thus took off under the best of auspices, also because the young composer from Busseto had won—and not without effort—the esteem of the most prestigious cultural salons and institutes in Milan, succeeding in making his debut in one of Italy's leading theaters, in that way

the base of which there is a strong sense of rhythm, not only musical but also theatrical-dramatic, that contributes to the rapid pace of events. Certainly, the characters still have somewhat conventional qualities, but clearly present in the protagonist Oberto is that father figure emblematic of power, morality, and vigor that Verdi was to develop in many later works.

immediately making known his already unquestionable qualities as a composer.

Oberto is certainly an opera strongly structured according to the canons of melodrama of the Bellini and Donizetti type, but it already presents those accents, that vigor, and even the germ of many themes that were later present in a great many of the operas by Verdi. In this score one can already note that conciseness of language at

Oberto was reprised at La Scala in October 1840. For these performances Verdi wrote two new pieces and adapted the role of Riccardo to suit the needs of available performers. The same was done with a performance in Genoa in 1841, for which Verdi rewrote three pieces of the score. This disproves the common notion that Verdi was completely insensitive to the needs of singers and the demands of singing.

Above, top: Portrait of Antonio Barezzi, great patron and friend of Verdi.

Above, center: Piazza del Teatro alla Scala, Milan, as it appeared during the period of *Oberto*, in a painting by Angelo Inganni.

Un Giorno di Regno, ossia Il Finto Stanislao

Melodramma giocoso in two acts to a libretto by
Felice Romani, based on the play *Le Faux Stanislas*
by Alexandre-Vincent Pineu Duval

FIRST PERFORMANCE
TEATRO ALLA SCALA, MILAN, SEPTEMBER 5, 1840

FIRST PERFORMERS
ANTONIETTA MARINI-RAINIERI (MARCHESA DEL POGGIO), LUIGIA ABBADIA (GIULIETTA),
LORENZO SALVI (EDOARDO), RAFFAELE FERLOTTI (BELFIORE), RAFFAELE SCALESE
(BARON KELBAR), AGOSTINO ROVERE (LA ROCCA), GIUSEPPE VASCHETTI (COUNT IVREA),
NAPOLEONE MARCONI (DELMONTE)

CHARACTERS
Cavaliere di Belfiore, impersonating King Stanislaw of Poland (*baritone*)
Baron Kelbar (*comic bass*)
Marchesa del Poggio, the baron's niece, a young widow in love with Belfiore (*soprano*)
Giulietta di Kelbar, the baron's daughter, in love with Edoardo di Sanval (*mezzo-soprano*)
Edoardo di Sanval, young officer (*tenor*)
La Rocca, Edoardo's uncle and treasurer of the Estates of Brittany (*comic bass*)
Count Ivrea, commander of Brest (*tenor*)
Delmonte, squire of Belfiore (*bass*)

CHORUSES AND EXTRAS
Servants, chambermaids, vassals of the baron

TIME: 1733.
PLACE: The castle of Kelbar in the area of Brest, France.

Above: The theatrical impresario Bartolomeo Merelli. He directed theaters in St. Petersburg, Paris, London, and Berlin, but his headquarters was Milan's La Scala.

PLOT
Act I
The Cavaliere di Belfiore has assumed the identity of King Stanislaw I of Poland to permit the king to escape a plot and reclaim the throne. Under this false identity, Belfiore arrives at the castle of Baron Kelbar, where preparations are underway for two marriages, that of Giulietta to the great treasurer La Rocca and that of the marchesa of Poggio to Count Ivrea. Belfiore, in love with the marchesa, and fearful that she might reveal his false identity, dashes off a letter to the true Stanislaw, asking the king to relieve him of this onerous task.

The marchesa, meanwhile, to test Belfiore, pretends to consent to the wedding with the count. Belfiore, thanks to his disguise, decides to help the young Edoardo, in love with Giulietta, who in turn is supported by the marchesa. Belfiore has no trouble flattering the treasurer into aspiring to a more important position and a marriage with greater lineage; thus, at the moment of the marriage contract, the situation collapses. The furious baron challenges the treasurer to a duel. Belfiore intervenes and manages to momentarily calm the situation, and as king he takes it upon himself to resolve the dispute.

Act II
Following his plan designed to support the young Edoardo, Belfiore convinces the treasurer to give his nephew one of his castles, along with a large

income: he can thus aspire to the hand of Giulietta, in that way calming the baron, while the treasurer can marry a princess promised by the false Stanislaw. A little later, Belfiore and the marchesa find themselves face to face: Belfiore, continuing his fiction, feigns indifference, while the marchesa provokes him by making clear her firm intention to marry Count Ivrea. In the end the disappointed marchesa decides she'll marry Count Ivrea but only if Belfiore doesn't arrive within an hour. Meanwhile he has already put into action another move: Count Ivrea, for "reasons of state," must leave with him immediately, so the wedding cannot take place. Everything ends in the best of ways when the letter finally arrives from Poland announcing the recognition of the true Stanislaw. After joining Giulietta and Edoardo in marriage, Belfiore reveals his true identity and can thus reaffirm, amid general happiness, his love for the marchesa.

Far left: Baron Kelbar as performed by the baritone Alfonso Antoniozzi, Teatro Regio, Parma, 1997. Conducted by Maurizio Benini; direction, sets, and costumes by Pier Luigi Pizzi.

Below: The mezzo-soprano Fiorenza Cossotto performed the role of the Marchesa del Poggio in the recorded version of the opera in 1974, conducted by Lamberto Gardelli.

Left: The buffo baritone Bruno Praticò in the role of La Rocca, Teatro Regio, Parma, 1997.

Above: Detail of a portrait of Margherita Barezzi, Verdi's first wife, in a painting by Augusto Mussini.

Below, inset: The librettist, poet, and critic Felice Romani in a 19th-century engraving. He wrote nearly a hundred libretti, most of them for Bellini, but also for Donizetti, Rossini, and Verdi.

BACKGROUND AND ANALYSIS

We last saw Verdi in the full success of *Oberto*, a success that, as indicated, earned him the commission to write three operas to be performed at La Scala. La Scala's director, Bartolomeo Merelli, suggested to Verdi a libretto by Gaetano Rossi, author of several works for Rossini, such as *Tancredi* and *Semiramide*. The libretto chosen was *Il Proscritto*, but then Merelli suddenly realized that the program for La Scala's season was without an opera buffa, so he gave Verdi several libretti by Felice Romani, one of the most famous theatrical writers of his age. Verdi was not particularly enthusiastic but, in part because he too felt pressed for time, he agreed to *Il Finto Stanislao* (*The False Stanislaw*), which in his version

became *Un Giorno di Regno* (*King for a Day*). Based on a play by Duval, *Le Faux Stanislas*, which in turn had been based, equally freely, on historical events concerning the Polish King Stanislaw I Leszczynski (1677–1766), the libretto by Romani is chock-full of unresolved and incongruous elements.

It might come as a surprise to find that a composer like Verdi, gifted with so much innate theatrical instinct, agreed to write music for such an incoherent libretto without at least attempting to improve it or make adjustments. One can only suppose that this state of indifference was in large part brought about by the difficulties he was experiencing in his private life, afflicted by truly sorrowful events. Between 1838 and 1839 his children, a son and a daughter, both died. While he was working on the composition Verdi himself fell sick with angina and was cared for by his wife, Margherita Barezzi. A few weeks after he finally felt better, Margherita fell seriously ill and died of encephalitis.

In this state of mind Verdi finished work on *Un Giorno di Regno*, which had its opening on September 5, 1840.

FELICE ROMANI

Felice Romani (1788–1865), born in Genoa, was the most important librettist after Metastasio. He applied equal talent to every theatrical genre, from tragic to satiric, and became one of the poets most sought after by the leading composers of his time. For Rossini he wrote Il Turco in Italia, Bianca e Falliero, *and* Adina. *For Donizetti he wrote* Anna Bolena, L'Elisir d'Amore, Parisina, *and* Lucrezia Borgia. *However, his name is most associated with the operas of Bellini, for whom he wrote all the libretti except* I Puritani.

In his attention to the beauty of verses and his adherence to the formal construction of scenes, Romani reflected the theatrical style known as neoclassical, and he rejected Romantic aesthetics with their passions and recourse to the fantastic and irrational. This formal aspect of his work had

already seemed "old" to Donizetti, who abandoned Romani for Salvatore Cammarano, so it was "antique" when Romani met the young Verdi.

Romani was still a very active librettist (he wrote until 1855), and certainly had the aid of Merelli, La Scala's impresario, who still tried to avoid spending more than he had to on composers. In this case Romani did not give him an original libretto but rather Il Finto Stanislao, *which he'd written nearly twenty years earlier for the composer Adalbert Gyrowetz and which had been performed at La Scala in 1818 only to immediately vanish.*

Verdi's version, transformed into Un Giorno di Regno, *underwent damaging changes that rendered it at times devoid of logic. Unfortunately, there are no documents that might throw light on the relationship between Verdi and Romani.*

This did nothing to improve his state of mind: the opera was a complete fiasco. Five performances had been planned, but the first was also the last. A great deal has been written about the reasons behind this large-scale failure: the quality of the execution, somewhat inferior, according to period witnesses, or the quality of the music, its lack of originality, too close to the style of Rossini and Donizetti. One can only affirm that once again, with this, his second work, Verdi set himself apart from his predecessors. He did not set out as a wide-ranging composer, able to move from genre to genre, but he clearly wasn't lacking in talent, just as he certainly wasn't lacking in technical ability. The route that Verdi followed had been opened by *Oberto*; *Un Giorno di Regno* can be seen as a sort of parenthesis to which Verdi was destined to return, under far different circumstances, nearly half a century later with *Falstaff*.

Three moments from the opera as presented at Parma's Teatro Regio in 1997. Among the performers are the sopranos Cecilia Gasdia and Anna Caterina Antonacci, the tenor Cesare Catani, and the baritone Paolo Coni.

Nabucco

Dramma lirico in four parts
to a libretto by Temistocle Solera

FIRST PERFORMANCE
TEATRO ALLA SCALA, MILAN, MARCH 9, 1842

FIRST PERFORMERS
GIUSEPPINA STREPPONI (ABIGAILLE), GIOVANNINA BELLINZAGHI (FENENA),
TERESA RUGGERI (ANNA), CORRADO MIRAGLIA (ISMAELE),
GIORGIO RONCONI (NABUCCO), PROSPER DÉRIVIS (ZACCARIA),
NAPOLEONE MARCONI (ABDALLO), GAETANO ROSSI (HIGH PRIEST OF BAAL)

CHARACTERS

Nabucco (Nebuchadnezzar), king of Babylon (*baritone*)

Ismaele, nephew of Sedecia, the king of Jerusalem (*tenor*)

Zaccaria, high priest of the Hebrews (*bass*)

Abigaille, a slave, believed to be the firstborn daughter of Nabucco (*soprano*)

Fenena, daughter of Nabucco (*soprano*)

The High Priest of Baal (*bass*)

Abdallo, an elderly officer of the king of Babylon (*tenor*)

Anna, Zaccaria's sister (*soprano*)

CHORUSES AND EXTRAS
Babylonian and Hebrew soldiers, Levites, Hebrew virgins, Babylonian women, magi, lords of the kingdom of Babylon, populace

TIME: 586 BC.
PLACE: Jerusalem and Babylon.

PLOT

Part I—Jerusalem

Inside the Temple of Solomon. The Hebrews raise heartfelt prayers to God to be saved from the Babylonians (also called the Assyrians in the libretto), who are advancing on Jerusalem, led by Nabucco. Zaccaria encourages the dismayed souls: he is accompanied by Fenena, Nabucco's daughter, a valuable hostage who might rein in the Babylonian king. Ismaele, nephew of the king of the Jews, is secretly in love with Fenena; when he was ambassador in Babylon she saved him from prison. Now, out of gratitude, Ismaele is determined to free her. Assyrian

soldiers disguised as Jews burst in, led by Abigaille, believed to be the first-born daughter of Nabucco. Abigaille, long infatuated with Ismaele, promises him salvation for his people provided he return her love. Ismaele refuses. The Jews pour back toward the Temple, followed by the soldiers. Immediately after, Nabucco enters, followed by the bulk of his army. Zaccaria grabs a dagger and tries to strike Fenena; but Ismaele intervenes, stopping his hand. Now that he sees his daughter freed, Nabucco orders the sack of Jerusalem.

Part II—The Impious One

Apartments in the royal palace of Babylon. Abigaille has managed to take possession of a parchment from which she learns she was born to a slave, not the king. Even so she has no

On these pages, clockwise from opposite top left: Giuseppe Verdi in 1843 in an oil painting by Torriani.

The soprano Giuseppina Strepponi, first interpreter of Abigaille, shown with the score of the opera in a painting made after 1842.

Title page of the score of *Nabucodonosor* (*Nabucco*), with a dedication to Adelaide of Austria, first wife of Victor Emmanuel II.

Francesco Hayez, *Destruction of the Temple of Jerusalem*, 1867, Gallerie dell'Accademia, Venice.

The Bulgarian soprano Ghena Dimitrova, one of the most authoritative interpreters of Abigaille, in a 1991 production of the opera at the Arena in Verona.

In that way she will be able to assume the crown and exterminate the Jews.

Fenena, meanwhile, is about to convert to the Hebrew religion, and Zaccaria, on his way to her, calls on God for support in his mission. Meanwhile, news of the death of Nabucco is spreading; Abigaille, with the support of priests, is ready to assume power. Amid the general confusion and terror, Nabucco bursts in. To reaffirm his power he insists he should be worshiped as a god: he is struck by a lightning bolt. Amid the general dismay, the king shows signs of madness. Abigaille takes the crown and puts it on her head.

intention of giving up her plans to take power and plots with the High Priest of Baal to kill Fenena and spread false news of the death of Nabucco in battle.

Part III—The Prophecy

Nabucco is crazed and thus Abigaille has herself proclaimed queen; she also manages to get the royal seal from the

delirious Nabucco and with it she condemns to death all the Jews, including Fenena, converted to their faith. The Jews, chained and condemned to forced labor, lament their sorrowful fate and remember with nostalgia their distant homeland ("Va, pensiero"). Zaccaria arrives, prophesying the end of their enslavement and the destruction of Babylon.

Part IV—The Broken Idol

Imprisoned in his rooms, Nabucco sees his daughter in chains as she, along with other condemned Jews, is led to the site of her execution. Instinctively Nabucco prays to the god of the Jews, imploring pardon. The madness that had darkened his mind suddenly vanishes; sword in hand, and in the company of Abdallo and his faithful followers, he rushes to save Fenena. In front of the altar of Baal, Fenena, comforted by Zaccaria, prepares to die; but Nabucco arrives and saves her and the Jews. The image of

Above: Sketch for Part II of *Nabucco* by Mauro Carosi, Teatro alla Scala, Milan, 1986–87 season.

Left: Title page of the first piano score of *Nabucco*.

Baal collapses. Nabucco and all present exalt the power of the true God. Supported by two warriors, Abigaille is brought forward; she has poisoned herself, and before dying she asks forgiveness of Fenena and expresses the hope that her union with Ismaele will go well.

BACKGROUND AND ANALYSIS

After the fiasco of *Un Giorno di Regno*, the impresario Bartolomeo Merelli hastily removed the opera from La Scala's playbill and, as though hoping to redeem poor Verdi, reproposed *Oberto*. The response to this revival did not resemble the enthusiasm awakened by the first performance. The *Corriere delle Dame* of October 20, 1840, wrote: "The music, most especially in the first act, seems to many less vivacious this year than it was last year." Verdi, increasingly prey to states of physical collapse, had his furniture sent to Busseto, having determined to leave Milan and give up his activity as a composer.

Once again Merelli had a hand in events, offering Verdi a new libretto by Solera; from then on, the story of the birth of *Nabucco* meanders between legend and reality. Anecdotes give its genesis a kind of miraculous quality, beginning with Verdi's nearly accidental reading of the famous "Va, pensiero," inspiring him to work on the score. As he himself reported, he took the libretto home and tossed it on the table "with an almost violent gesture... In falling, it had opened of itself; without my realizing it, my eyes clung to the open page and to one special line: 'Va, pensiero, sull'ali dorate'" ("Fly, thought, on golden wings").

There are other stories, and whether they are factual or not, the composition of *Nabucco* went ahead at a rapid pace. Verdi had regained his usual feisty spirit, and with the lucidity and determination that were so important to his character he got the timid Solera to make changes in the plot of the libretto. In the end, the premiere of *Nabucco*, on March 9, 1842, was triumphant and represented, in the words of Verdi himself, "the beginning of my artistic career."

Contributing to that success, and not in a secondary way, were such phrases as "Do not let the Assyrian enemy sit on David's throne among his false idols!" or, even more, "In your servants light a breath of fire that will give death to the enemy." Speaking of foreigners, of a homeland, and of oppression in a Milan ruled by Austrians meant inflaming souls, and the addition of vibrant, passionate music flowing beneath the words certainly assured success. But what stands out most in *Nabucco* is not just Verdi the warrior or patriot, for beside that is ample room for more introspective sentiments, those closest to Verdian sensibilities: nostalgia, sorrow, defeat.

In truth, *Oberto* and *Un Giorno di Regno* seem light-years away from *Nabucco*. Everything in the score has a new, more vivid dimension. It is striking in its solemnity, which could be called biblical, and which is expressed in the chorus, a true protagonist. The chorus no longer represents simple connective episodes but forms true choral frescoes, from the initial "Gli arredi festivi" ("The festive decorations") to "Va, pensiero," famously described by Rossini as "a great aria for sopranos, altos, tenors, and basses." Verdi's peremptory, almost harsh language, which points directly to a strict dramatic-theatrical functionality, finds full expression here: the use of recitative, perfectly molded to events and psychological character description, is the most striking result of this effort. Along with what we would call the chorus-character, Verdi paints Zaccaria and Nabucco with great intuition, producing fully formed characters that anticipate later Verdian developments. There remains the uniqueness of Abigaille, an impetuous female, gritty and almost ironic in her spasmodic thirst for power, rendered by Verdi in sharp, biting tones that clearly portray her inevitably self-destructive character.

Opposite: Costumes by Odette Nicoletti for Nabucco and Ismaele in the La Scala production of the 1986–87 season. Conducted by Riccardo Muti, directed by Roberto De Simone. Principal performers: Renato Bruson (Nabucco), Ghena Dimitrova (Abigaille), Paata Burchuladze (Zaccaria).

Below: A scene from the opera in the 1972 production at the Teatro La Fenice, Venice.

I Lombardi alla Prima Crociata

Dramma lirico in four acts to a libretto by
Temistocle Solera, based on the poem *I Lombardi
alla Prima Crociata* by Tommaso Grossi

FIRST PERFORMANCE
TEATRO ALLA SCALA, MILAN, FEBRUARY 11, 1843

FIRST PERFORMERS
ERMINIA FREZZOLINI (GISELDA), TERESA RUGGERI (VICLINDA),
CARLO GUASCO (ORONTE), GIOVANNI SEVERI (ARVINO),
PROSPER DÉRIVIS (PAGANO), GAETANO ROSSI (PIRRO),
NAPOLEONE MARCONI (PRIOR OF MILAN)

CHARACTERS

Arvino, son of Folco, lord of Rò (*tenor*)

Pagano, his brother (*bass*)

Viclinda, Arvino's wife (*soprano*)

Giselda, her daughter (*soprano*)

Pirro, Arvino's squire (*bass*)

Prior of the city of Milan (*tenor*)

Acciano, tyrant of Antioch (*bass*)

Oronte, his son (*tenor*)

Sofia, Acciano's wife (*soprano*)

CHORUSES AND EXTRAS
Nuns; priors; populace; ruffians; armigers in Folco's palace; ambassadors from Persia, Media, Damascus, and Chaldea; harem women; Crusaders

TIME: 1099.
PLACE: Milan (Act I), Antioch and its surroundings (Acts II and III), and the environs of Jerusalem (Act IV).

PLOT

Act I—Revenge

Milan, the square in front of the church of Sant'Ambrogio. The crowd assembled in front of the cathedral rejoices at the reconciliation between the two sons of Folco, Arvino and Pagano. Years ago, Pagano was rejected by Viclinda, who preferred and married his brother. Blinded by jealousy, Pagano tried to kill his brother, for which he was exiled. Now the two brothers have been reconciled, although doubts concerning the sincerity of Pagano's repentance trouble the bystanders. Meanwhile the prior announces a crusade to liberate Jerusalem; Arvino will lead the Lombards. After everyone else has gone away, Pagano, with the complicity of Pirro, reveals his intention to abduct Viclinda.

The scene moves to Folco's palace. It is night. Pagano enters furtively and, after stealing into his brother's room to kill him, returns on the scene bearing the bloody dagger and dragging Viclinda. Arvino, Giselda, and servants rush in. After a momentary stupor, Pagano realizes he has killed his father. He desperately tries to kill himself but is restrained by those present; he faces another exile along with the weight of this new blow.

Act II—The Man of the Cave

Antioch, a room in Acciano's palace. The tyrant receives the announcement that the Crusaders are advancing. After invoking the wrath of Allah on the invaders, all leave. Acciano's wife, Sofia, arrives with their son Oronte. The youth laments his unhappy love for a Christian girl, Giselda, prisoner in the harem. For his love Oronte is prepared to convert to Christianity. He is encouraged by his mother, who has already secretly converted.

The scene shifts to the mouth of a cave in the side of a mountain. This is the home of the hermit Pagano. He anxiously awaits the arrival of the Crusaders, eager to help them liberate Jerusalem. A little later, to the sound of a march, here come the Lombards with Arvino in the lead. Pagano, wearing a helmet to avoid being recognized, joins the Crusaders on their way toward Antioch, where Giselda is being held prisoner. In the harem, meanwhile, Giselda weeps over her sorrowful fate: she is a prisoner and she's in love with an infidel. Just then the Crusaders burst in, led by Arvino and the hermit. Arvino and his daughter are reunited. The blood on Arvino's clothing awakens horror in his daughter: God would never want so much blood to be shed.

Act III—The Conversion

In the valley of Jehoshaphat, not far from Jerusalem. Near the Lombard camp Giselda sees Oronte, whom she had believed dead. The two decide to flee, but Oronte, followed by Crusaders, is mortally wounded. Nearly dead and supported by Giselda, he finds refuge in a cave near the Jordan. Here too is Pagano, who baptizes him. Dying, Oronte promises Giselda that one day they will be together in heaven.

Act IV—The Holy Sepulcher

Lombard camp. Giselda sees her beloved Oronte in a dream in which he shows her how to reach the water that will refresh the thirsty troops. Their thirst finally quenched, the Lombards throw themselves into battle. The hermit is seriously wounded. Taken to a tent, he reveals his identity—Pagano—to Giselda and Arvino. Forgiven by his brother and by God, he dies serenely, gazing at Jerusalem, over which flies the Crusader flag.

BACKGROUND AND ANALYSIS

Concerning the birth of *I Lombardi alla Prima Crociata* (*The Lombards on the First Crusade*), chronicles narrate that during the second performance of *Nabucco*, Verdi received the usual visit from Merelli, who presented him with a contract missing both the signature and the fee. Verdi asked Strepponi how much he should ask for a new opera, and she responded, "What Bellini asked for *Norma*. You're worth it! Eight thousand Austrian lire" (then the most ever paid for an opera). Verdi made the request and got the contract, for the first time proving himself able to demand high sums. He then prepared to compose *I Lombardi*.

Opposite, top: Scenery for *I Lombardi alla Prima Crociata*, by Mario Sironi, 1948.

Opposite, bottom: French illustration from the 13th century depicting a small group of auxiliaries setting up a tent for Crusader knights.

Perhaps fearful of taking false steps, for this new opera Verdi again turned to Temistocle Solera. After *Oberto*, and most of all the success of *Nabucco*, it was important for Verdi to avoid risking changes. It is immediately clear that the dramatic outline of *I Lombardi* closely follows that of *Nabucco*. It too has four parts, each with a subtitle, each of brief duration, with the large-scale presence

Above: A scene from *I Lombardi* in the 1984 production at the Teatro alla Scala. Conducted by Gianandrea Gavazzeni, directed by Gabriele Lavia.

JÉRUSALEM

The dramatic outline of the French version parallels the original in so many ways that the score did not require notable changes. Even so, there are new pieces, beginning with the introduction, followed by a brief duet between Gaston and Hélène. This is followed by an instrumental piece, a charming musical depiction of the rising sun. New Act II pieces include the march and a chorus of Crusaders with a terzetto by the Count, Roger, and Adhémar de Monteil. In Act III Verdi inserted a ballet, an obligatory piece for Paris. This act includes the most interesting piece in Jérusalem, the judgment and condemnation of Gaston, which has notable theatrical power and anticipates the judgment scene in Aida. The last act includes a very beautiful orchestral passage that describes the battle for the conquest of Jerusalem.

This opera, Verdi's first experience working outside his usual borders, did not prove especially successful; in fact, the reception given Jérusalem by the Parisian public was anything but enthusiastic, although the same was not true of its reception in other French theaters, where it was embraced with greater conviction. Verdi's relationship with the French public, and even more so with the nearly ironclad rules to which a musician had to submit when taking on the French theaters, was somewhat difficult and remained so for the works still to come.

A few years later the French text of Jérusalem was translated into Italian and presented under the title Gerusalemme at Milan's La Scala as the opening work of the 1850–51 season; on this occasion too, the work was received with little enthusiasm.

This Italian version of the opera was presented in 1963 at Venice's La Fenice, and the French version was performed in an Italian RAI radio/TV production in Turin (1975) in the form of a concert and in the staged form in the same city at the Teatro Regio (1995).

Above: The American soprano Aprile Millo, acclaimed interpreter of Giselda at Carnegie Hall in 1984, played the role again at New York's Metropolitan Opera in 1993, with Luciano Pavarotti under the direction of James Levine.

of the chorus and a variety of scene changes. This dramatic-musical structure was designed to ensure a positive outcome. Also clearly in evidence was the political message: in Nabucco there are the oppressed Hebrews; here are the valorous Lombards who free Jerusalem from the infidels. The true meaning was clear: the desire to free Milan from the Austrians. The libretto by the fervent patriot Solera did not lack such references and incitements.

Once again the Milanese public proved as responsive as ever to the message, and the work's success on February 11, 1843, was even greater than that of Nabucco. However, the critics expressed less enthusiasm, immediately highlighting the incongruities of the libretto and a certain discontinuity of inspiration in Verdi's music. In effect, I Lombardi lacks the perfect balance between drama and musical language, that close rhythm that is so characteristic of Nabucco. The chorus also lost the primary role it had in the preceding opera. In I Lombardi the chorus returns to being an almost sideline element, relegated to a narration that is often conventional. The characters seem more stereotypical and are hardly convincing dramatically. As for the music, moments of pure theatrical functionality alternate with those in which all of the composer's genius shines forth.

Standing out among the opera's most important moments are the refined har-

monies and sweetness of Giselda's "Salve Maria" prayer in Act I and the great conversion scene in Act III, with a magnificent adagio for violin and orchestra that characterizes the entire terzetto and that transforms the piece into a sort of splendid trio concertante. Also splendid is the Lombards' chorus "O Signore, dal tetto natio" ("O Lord, who called us from our native home"), a beautifully worked piece that suffers only from its marked resemblance to the other opera's "Va, pensiero" chorus.

In this uneven opera, the banal and the sublime travel as a pair. These aspects have partially marked the fortune of *I Lombardi*, a fortune that certainly differs from that of *Nabucco*, which has never left the repertoire. With the passage of time, instead, a certain lack of interest has fallen on *I Lombardi*, and the work has gradually been relegated to the margins of the great lyrical repertoire. This decline in appreciation dates primarily to the 20th century, for during the 19th *I Lombardi* was performed a little everywhere; year, thus never managing to enjoy what became a vital condition for him: the ability to freely compose, dedicating the necessary time to every opera, without constrictions from impresarios or directors. But this phase of his career can be read another way. It was a sort of "voluntary exile," of vigorous "field" training, a sort of "theatrical practice ground" to which the young Verdi surrendered to refine his musical-dramatic style and language. "Galley years" because consciously or not, the sense of being first and foremost an artist became an increasing reality in Verdi, along with the

Above: The novelist and poet Tommaso Grossi, author of the poem *I Lombardi alla Prima Crociata* (1826).

Left: Scene from a La Scala production of *I Lombardi alla Prima Crociata*. Conducted by Gianandrea Gavazzeni, directed by Gabriele Lavia, sets by Giovanni Agostinucci, costumes by Andrea Viotto.

indeed, it was the first Verdi opera to be performed in the United States, at Palmo's Opera House in New York, on March 3, 1847. In that same year Verdi reworked the score for the Paris Opéra, where it was performed under the title *Jérusalem*.

With *I Lombardi* we enter the long period of hard work Verdi called his "galley years," the nine years between *Nabucco* (1842) and *Rigoletto* (1851), when he wrote one and sometimes two operas a desire to express himself without outside influence. It was a freedom to defend at all costs. During his work on *I Lombardi* Verdi had the first of a long series of confrontations with censors. The archbishop of Milan wanted to eliminate Oronte's baptism in Act III, but Verdi was adamant; his only concession was to change Giselda's prayer in Act I from "Ave Maria" to "Salve Maria." It was the first victory for a young but already fierce composer!

Ernani

Dramma lirico in four acts to a libretto
by Francesco Maria Piave, based on the play
Hernani, ou l'Honneur Castillan by Victor Hugo

FIRST PERFORMANCE
TEATRO LA FENICE, VENICE, MARCH 9, 1844

FIRST PERFORMERS
SOPHIE LOEWE (ELVIRA), CARLO GUASCO (ERNANI),
ANTONIO SUPERCHI (DON CARLO), ANTONIO SELVA (SILVA)

CHARACTERS

Ernani, the bandit (*tenor*)
Don Carlo, king of Spain (*baritone*)
Don Ruy Gomez de Silva, a Spanish grandee (*bass*)
Elvira, his niece and betrothed (*soprano*)
Giovanna, her nurse (*soprano*)
Don Riccardo, the king's squire (*tenor*)
Jago, Silva's squire (*bass*)

CHORUSES AND EXTRAS
Rebel mountaineers and bandits, knights and members of Silva's household, Elvira's handmaids, knights of the king, members of the League, Spanish and German nobles, Spanish and German ladies, electors and grandees of the imperial court, pages, German soldiers

TIME: 1519.
PLACE: In the Pyrenees and Silva's castle (Acts I and II), Aix-la-Chapelle (Act III), and Saragossa (Act IV).

PLOT

Act I—The Bandit

The bandit Ernani, really Don Giovanni of Aragon, pretender to the throne of Spain, tells his companions he loves the noblewoman Elvira and asks for help in abducting her and thus saving her from an undesired marriage with her uncle and tutor Gomez de Silva.

In Silva's castle, Elvira awaits Ernani; Don Carlo (King Charles V) of Spain loves her and manages to furtively enter her apartments, where he again declares his passion. Elvira rejects him, grabs his dagger, and points it at her chest. Ernani puts himself between them and confronts his rival. Then the old Silva enters, eager to avenge his wounded pride. When he recognizes the king, he calms and agrees to host Carlo for the night; the king declares that Ernani is one of his followers (thus saving the bandit for the king's own revenge) and insists that he immediately leave the castle to get away from Silva's anger. Ernani does indeed depart, promising Elvira he will return and save her.

Act II—The Guest

In a hall of Silva's castle. Preparations are underway for the wedding of Elvira and the elderly Silva. Ernani arrives too, disguised as a pilgrim, and asks hospitality of Silva, who welcomes him and reconfirms his hospitality even when Ernani, seeing Elvira ready for the wedding and believing himself betrayed, reveals his identity. A squire announces the arrival of the king and his men; Silva again delays his plans of revenge and leads Ernani to a hiding place to avoid the searches of the king, always on the trail of his enemy and rival. Don Carlo has indeed followed Ernani, and now, when Silva refuses to hand over the bandit, the king orders a search of the castle and, when nothing is found, he leaves, taking Elvira as a valuable hostage. When all have left, Ernani tells

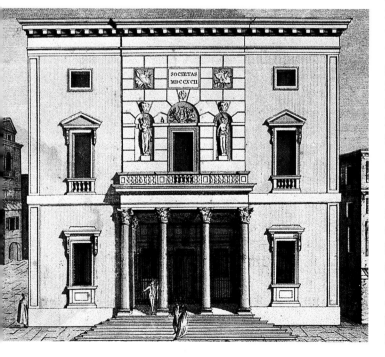

Silva that the king too loves Elvira. Ernani exhorts the nobleman to assist him against Carlo; then, when Silva wishes, Ernani will submit to his revenge. To seal this pact he gives Silva a hunting horn, saying that when Silva sounds the horn, Ernani will kill himself.

Act III—Clemency

Aix-la-Chapelle, the burial vault of Charlemagne. Carlo has heard of a con-

plotters, but Elvira arrives and begs for clemency. The new emperor pardons all of them and pushes Elvira into the arms of Ernani, returning to him his noble titles. Only the old Silva does not join in the general joy, prepared as he is to carry out his vendetta.

Act IV—The Mask

Ernani has resumed his true identity and celebrates his wedding to Elvira in his

spiracy and wants to surprise the plotters, among them Ernani and Silva, who have sworn to kill him on the day he is proclaimed emperor. Unseen, he hides in a crypt, and from there he gets confirmation of the criminal plan; when three cannon shots announce his election, he shows himself to the conspirators, who try in vain to flee. In the same instant the portal of the underground chamber opens and the scene fills with the leading men of the kingdom, followed by ladies and gentlemen. Carlo orders the arrest and condemnation to death of the

palace. But a sinister figure lurks among the guests, wrapped in a black domino: the old Silva. Finally alone, Elvira and Ernani think of past sorrow and present happiness. But the night's silence is broken by the fatal horn call. Ernani understands immediately, but Elvira cannot explain his sudden anguish. Then Silva appears, implacable, and presents Ernani with poison and a dagger, letting him choose. Faithful to his vow, Ernani stabs himself, dying in the arms of the desperate Elvira, who throws herself on his lifeless body.

Above: The baritone Renato Bruson (Don Carlo) and the bass Roberto Scandiuzzi (Silva) in a production of Verdi's opera at the Teatro La Fenice, Venice, 1990.

BACKGROUND AND ANALYSIS

Performances of *I Lombardi* began in February 1843; a month later Verdi was conquering new stages. Thanks to the unconditional support of the illustrious composer Gaetano Donizetti, Verdi brought *Nabucco* to Vienna's Kärntnertor Theater, where Donizetti conducted two performances to great success.

In Italy, meanwhile, Venice's Teatro La Fenice was showing great interest in the young composer. Verdi responded positively to the summons from the Venetian theater, but he was also more determined than ever to get a fair price for his work. From the 8,000 Austrian lire asked of La Scala for *I Lombardi*, Verdi, demonstrating skill as his own manager, asked Count Alvise Mocenigo,

The Battle of Hernani, painting by Paul Albert Besnard, 1909, shows the first 1830 performance of Hugo's play and makes clear the stormy response of the "classicists" in opposition to the Romantics, led by Théophile Gautier, showing off his signature red vest.

president of La Fenice, for the impressive sum of 12,000 lire. To Mocenigo's timid protestations, Verdi firmly replied, "Next year I'd ask more!"

So it was that Verdi got his contract. Now under pressure to come up with a subject for the new opera, he found himself undecided. Two plays by Byron interested him, *The Two Foscari* and *The Bride of Abydos*, but he was drawn just as

strongly to Shakespeare's *King Lear*, a project he was destined to return to various times without ever succeeding in bringing it to a conclusion. In the end, Verdi's attention came to rest on the French author Victor Hugo, and more precisely on that man's play *Hernani, ou l'Honneur Castillan* (*Ernani, or Castilian Honor*), which had been performed with great success in Paris in 1830 and had become the public "manifesto" of the new Romantic literature in French culture. Verdi sensed the dramatic force of Hugo's drama, its tragedy, which was an important element to add to his dramatic expression and in years to come would gradually lead him to Byron, Schiller, and the much-loved Shakespeare.

With clear ideas as to how the opera should develop, Verdi accepted a thirty-year-old librettist from the Venetian island of Murano, Francesco Maria

Francesco Hayez, *Combatant of the Cinque Giornate*, Museo del Risorgimento, Milan. This participant in the anti-Austrian uprising wears an "Ernani-style" hat, much in vogue at the time.

Piave, who was the jack-of-all-trades at the Teatro La Fenice: proofreader, assistant to the scenery director, publicist, poet. Verdi intuited his great abilities as well as his total in-experience, which offered Verdi the pos-sibility of being able to do with Piave more or less whatever he wanted. And that, of course, is exactly what happened: Piave proved ductile material in the hands of the willful mae-stro, who buried the poor librettist in requests. In the end, the opera was performed to success, but Verdi was

Left, inset: The famous Parma baritone Gaetano Ferri dressed as Don Carlo in *Ernani*.

Below: The baritone Renato Bruson and the soprano Mirella Freni in the produc-tion of *Ernani* that inaugu-rated the 1982–83 season at Milan's La Scala. Conducted by Riccardo Muti, directed by Luca Ronconi, sets by Ezio Frigerio, costumes by Franca Squarciapino.

in no sense content, because the singers had given a mediocre performance. As he wrote, "Yesterday we heard *Ernani* with Guasco without a voice and appallingly hoarse. It is not possi-ble to sing more false notes than did Loewe. All the pieces, some more than others, were applauded, with the excep-tion of Guasco's cavatina."

Even so, *Ernani* enjoyed increasing success and almost triumph in its reprise, two months later, at the Teatro San Benedetto, where it received its definitive consecration. The dramatic-

Left: *Ernani*, Act IV, the end of the opera, in the 1970 production at Rome's Teatro dell'Opera.

Below, inset: The young Victor Hugo in a portrait by Jean Alaux, 1825.

musical relationship in *I Lombardi* lacked homogeneity, but in *Ernani* the relationships between action and music and between libretto and melodic invention worked to perfection. Verdi looked at the drama with great lucidity and fixed its points, what he referred to as the "positions," meaning the relationships and conflicts that animate the characters; he then cut away everything that was useless, that slowed down or distracted from the fulcrum of the action. Hugo's drama is based on continuous plot twists and on characters that burst onto the stage from hiding places, secret doors, and so forth. With Piave's help, Verdi translated these theatrical effects into music and constructed a mechanism in which the recitative was more or less nonexistent or reduced to the minimum so as to leave room for duets, trios, quartets, and concertati that together form a series of rapid-fire scenes that create true "plot twists."

Ernani is without doubt Verdi's first authentically Romantic opera; but it is an extreme Romanticism, almost rough, that can seem almost naïve in its leaps, and it is perhaps this aspect that makes it even today engaging and vital to the listener.

VICTOR HUGO

With his vast literary output, Victor Hugo (1802–1885) created many subjects for melodrama, beginning with Notre-Dame de Paris *(1831)*. Works by Hugo fashioned into operas include Marion Delorme *(1831), made into an opera by Ponchielli (1885);* Lucrezia Borgia *(1833) by Donizetti (1833);* Marie Tudor *(1836) by Pacini (1843); and* Angelo, Tyran de Padoue *(1835), made into* Il Giuramento *by Mercadante (1837) and* La Gioconda *by Ponchielli (1876).*

Verdi drew inspiration from Hugo in both Hernani *(1830) and* Le Roi S'Amuse *(1832), which became* Rigoletto. *How much was Verdi like Hugo? In "The 'Vulgarity' of Giuseppe Verdi" (*Man as an End and Other Essays*), Alberto Moravia writes, "The resemblance is only superficial. Hugo was a real European romantic—from him we come right to the decadents, to Baudelaire and Rimbaud; whereas Verdi's apparent romanticism leads to no similar decadence. And there is another difference between Verdi and Hugo: the latter believed in history, and that history determined men's conduct. As a result, the characters in Hugo's plays must be medieval men, or* Renaissance men, before they are men at all, so Hugo's plays are now unreadable and unplayable. Verdi's conception of history was immobile, static, humanistic, Plutarchian. And so his characters still interest us today, because they are first and foremost men, and only then medieval or Renaissance men." *What Moravia calls "decadence" was called "verismo" (realism) in Italy. Can the characters in* Ernani *really be called men and women in the absolute sense? Massimo Mila says the young Verdi carried out an operation of a critical nature, an analysis of humanity, of psychology, of how life enriches and impoverishes souls. He would first discover this life fully in* Rigoletto. *But now, Mila stresses, he was still sharpening his weapons: "It is clear that characters so isolated from every atmospheric setting risk looking like ridiculous puppets, helpless abstractions . . . And Ernani, Elvira, Silva, and Carlo are puppets in their tragicomic jealousies, their demented amorous manias."*

Two very different views with which one can decide to agree or not to agree.

Above and opposite: Two details of a postcard dedicated to *Ernani*, a Verdian opera that enjoyed great fame over the course of the 19th century.

[. . .] *Ernani* was the first of the five operas Giuseppe Verdi wrote expressly for the Teatro La Fenice of Venice. The subject, taken with few changes from Victor Hugo (*Hernani, ou l'Honneur Castillan*, a poetic drama first performed in Paris in 1830), was chosen after much indecision and reconsideration and at the express wish of Verdi.

Taking advantage of the inability to employ his usual librettist, Temistocle Solera, Verdi himself prepared the dramatization of the work and entrusted the novice librettist Francesco Maria Piave with little more than the role of mere versifier. The subject was not new to the operatic theater stage; in 1832 Vincenzo Bellini had begun composition of his own *Ernani*, using a libretto by Felice Romani, a project later abandoned because of a veto from censors. Lines created for it were later adapted to *La Sonnambula*. Hugo's play had an irresistible fascination, especially because of its violent Romantic force and its great variety of plot twists. The demonstrations set off by performances of Hugo's play, beginning with its first performance in Paris, were well known. Seen as an example of the most flagrant Romanticism, it quickly became a kind of "manifesto" of bourgeois nonconformism. Verdi's insistence in arguing with the directors of La Fenice to get them to choose *Hernani* suggests he already had a certain intuition of the subject's melodramatic promise. In fact, Verdi was trying to move away from the formula so perfectly rendered in *Nabucco* and repeated in *I Lombardi* to direct himself toward a new concept of melodra-

ma, one more in keeping with his sensibilities and with the desires of his public: the opera based on character. No longer would the protagonist be the chorus-crowd, replaced instead by a few well-sculpted characters on whom the drama would be concentrated. Unlike the arrangement in *Nabucco* and *I Lombardi*, the chorus would assume a decorative and theatrical function, almost abdicating its major dramatic role. The absence of a good librettist combined with such a sprawling subject, packed with events and plot twists, probably prevented Verdi from enriching and further delineating the characters to give them greater depth.

Verdi's desire to turn *Ernani* into a "love" opera may have had a negative effect, since Hugo had originally conceived it to give prevalent emphasis to the theme of honor. But there is no doubt that Verdi intended to put love in the foreground. If further proof were needed it would suffice to observe the melody that appears in the initial prelude; it is the same melody that we encounter in Act IV when the two lovers, having finished the celebration, move toward the nuptial bower and Ernani sings, "Ve' come gli astri stessi, Elvira mia, sorrider" ("See how the stars themselves are smiling, my Elvira"). The way Verdi so clearly emphasizes this theme, which underlines the brief moment of the two lovers' happiness, indicates that he deliberately wanted to present the love of the two youths as the central motif of the work. In truth, Hugo's drama offered little in the way of character traits that might fully respond to Verdi's melodramatic concept as it was to be developed over the coming years. In their desperate

cathartic development. As a result we find ourselves facing static figures that cannot evolve in response to the development of the drama. Their agitations in the face of the multiple vicissitudes of the strange events are completely superficial.

Perhaps it was precisely for that reason that even musically none of these four characters manages to emerge as a psychologically delineated figure with authentic depth. But Verdi was fascinated by this story, and with astonishing plot twists, disguises, apparitions, vows, nuptial feasts, and dances to stimulate his musical inventiveness, he managed to give this drama a singularly gripping idealization.

The lapidary conciseness of the stage presentation and the sharp definition of the characters correspond to an equally violent and peremptory musical inspiration. Perhaps Verdi himself made an effort in this regard to make his musical powers adequate to this type of drama of extroversion, so striking and full of chiaroscuro effects, often emphatically charged. We are first shown the figure of Ernani when, at the beginning of the opera, Verdi sketches in the delicacy of his feelings for Elvira using the minimum of lines to then immediately transform those feelings into apprehensions and hatred for the old Silva. Only rarely does Elvira's character manage to acquire the psychological depth necessary to justify not only Ernani's love but the passions of Silva and Carlo. Her vocal part—very likely influenced by the first performer of the role, Loewe—is

tions of the better known Verdian heroines. The "villain" of the drama, Silva, although a static figure dramatically, has a singular musical identity, with expressive vividness. Don Carlo unleashes greater musical force, even though with his relentless propensity for pardons and clemency his role risks declining to the level of a *deus ex machina*.

All this notwithstanding, *Ernani* has been and remains an opera of sure success: the inspired melodies with such exceptional penetrating force, the magniloquent dosage of the spectacular effects, and the shrewdly expressive instrumentation make a determinant contribution to the vitality of this opera. Added to this is the superior level of the composition of Act IV, in which the short act of happiness of the two youths is rapidly transformed into tragedy through a series of psychological passages logically connected one to the next and closely tied. On this subject we agree with Mila in seeing this number as among the greatest creations from the genius of Verdi. This is an opera of enormous interest for the opera-educated spectator, since it offers in a nutshell views of things that would become constants of Verdi's language, but even for the normal viewer it has interest for its inventive impetuosity and its potent Romanticism, two components that still awaken an unquestioned fascination. [...]

Adriano Cavicchi,
Guida all'Opera,
Arnoldo Mondadori Editore

I Due Foscari

Tragedia lirica in three acts
to a libretto by Francesco Maria Piave,
based on Lord Byron's play *The Two Foscari*

FIRST PERFORMANCE
TEATRO ARGENTINA, ROME, NOVEMBER 3, 1844

FIRST PERFORMERS
MARIANNA BARBIERI-NINI (LUCREZIA), GIULIA RICCI (PISANA),
GIACOMO ROPPA (JACOPO), ACHILLE DE BASSINI (FRANCESCO),
ATANASIO POZZOLINI (BARBARIGO), BALDASSARE MIRI (LOREDANO)

CHARACTERS

Francesco Foscari, octogenarian doge of Venice (*baritone*)

Jacopo Foscari, his son (*tenor*)

Lucrezia Contarini, Jacopo's wife (*soprano*)

Jacopo Loredano, member of the Council of Ten (*bass*)

Barbarigo, senator, member of the Giunta (*tenor*)

Pisana, Lucrezia's friend and confidante (*soprano*)

An official of the Council of Ten (*tenor*)

A servant of the doge (*bass*)

CHORUSES AND EXTRAS
Members of the Council of Ten and the Giunta, Lucrezia's maids, Venetian women, populace and masked figures of both sexes, the two small children of Jacopo Foscari, gondoliers, sailors, pages of the doge

TIME: 1457.
PLACE: Venice.

PLOT

Background Events

On April 15, 1423, Francesco Foscari is elected doge, and his direct adversary, Pietro Loredano, doesn't let an occasion pass for finding fault with his performance. During one of these altercations the doge inveighs against Loredano, crying out that he will never be able to be a true doge as long as Loredano is alive. A few months later, Pietro Loredano and his brother Marco are murdered. Pietro's son, Jacopo, convinced of Foscari's guilt, vows to get revenge. The doge's son, Jacopo, has been exiled for having had illegal relations with foreign rulers and is also accused of having had Ermolao Donato, the leader of the Council of Ten who had him condemned, killed. This new accusation increases the youth's sentence, and he must remain in exile for the rest of his life. Not accepting this unjust con-

demnation and desiring to prove his innocence, Jacopo sends a letter to the duke of Milan, Francesco Sforza, asking him to intercede with Venice. The letter is intercepted by the Council of Ten. Thus a new accusation of conspiracy against the republic hangs

over Jacopo Foscari, and he is brought back to Venice to again face trial.

Act I

Hall of the ducal palace. The Council of Ten is meeting to judge Jacopo Foscari. The young man is upset at the idea of having to appear in chains before his father and is afraid he will be unable to prove his innocence, given the hostility of the council, which has become even more evident since Jacopo Loredano has become one of its most influential members. In the Foscari palace, meanwhile, Lucrezia awaits in prayer the outcome of the judgment. Pisano enters to announce that the council has commuted the sentence from death to lifetime exile. Lucrezia decides to go to the doge to obtain the repeal of the sentence; he, in vain, tries to make her understand that his position prevents him from interfering in the decision of the Council of Ten.

Act II

In an underground cell, Jacopo, exhausted by his suffering, falls prey to delirious visions. Lucrezia arrives and announces the new sentence of exile; he cannot be accompanied by anyone, not his wife or his two children. The doge too arrives to say goodbye to his son and assure him of his affection.

Meanwhile Loredano arrives with some soldiers; with poorly concealed contempt he orders Jacopo to follow him to the hall of the council, where he will be given official notice of the sentence. In a scene of growing tension the sentence is read. Lucrezia bursts in with her children in a final attempt to convince the judges to let her accompany her husband. Every attempt is in vain; the council cannot change a decision it has made.

Act III

It is carnival, and groups of masked people crowd St. Mark's Square, while gondoliers race their gondolas. The festive atmosphere is interrupted by a gloomy procession: an armed guard escorts Jacopo toward the galley that will carry him into exile. Before getting on the ship Jacopo turns to give a last goodbye to his wife and children.

The scene changes. We are in the doge's apartments, where the old patrician weeps over the fate of the son he will never see again. Barbarigo enters greatly excited and announces that the noble Nicolò Erizzo, who is on the brink of death, has confessed to being the killer of Ermolao Donato, proving the innocence of Jacopo Foscari. The doge's joy lasts only a few moments, however; Lucrezia bring news that Jacopo, unable to bear the cruel separation from his dear ones, has died of sorrow.

The trials of the old man have not yet ended. Loredano wants to force Foscari to abdicate. The old doge tries to fight back, but in the end he surrenders and hands over the dogal emblems. The bells of St. Mark's announce the election of the new doge. Unable to bear this new humiliation, Francesco Foscari falls dead.

Opposite: The baritone Renato Bruson in costume as Doge Francesco Foscari in the 1988 production of the opera created by Pier Luigi Pizzi, Teatro alla Scala, Milan.

Above: Francesco Hayez, *The Parting of the Two Foscari*, 1852–54, Galleria d'Arte Moderna, Florence.

Left, inset: Portrait of Verdi from the period of *I Due Foscari*.

BACKGROUND AND ANALYSIS

The baritone Piero Cappuccilli as Doge Francesco Foscari.

Verdi had been drawn to Byron's play since its debut at La Fenice. "It is a fine subject, delicate, and very moving," he wrote to the librettist Piave. In a letter to Guglielmo Brenna, the theater's secretary, he described the subject as "full of passion and extremely well suited to being set to music," adding that it was also "a Venetian subject, which Venice might find very interesting." On the contrary, La Fenice's directors advised him to reconsider the subject to avoid hurting the feelings of the descendants of the Foscari and Loredano families. Verdi accepted this advice and turned his attention to Hugo's *Hernani*.

When he had completed that first engagement for Venice, Verdi, by then an established composer hailed by many as the heir to Donizetti, had to deal with another deadline for another new territory to conquer: Rome's Teatro Argentina. It was time to dust off Byron's *Two Foscari*. Verdi immediately involved the young Piave, and on May 9, 1844, he wrote, "I observe that in Byron there is none of the theatrical grandiosity that is needed by musical works. Torture your genius and find something that will make a big noise, especially in the first act." Piave went to work, and in a later letter of May 14 Verdi noted, "Fine drama, very beautiful, extremely beautiful. . . . I find the character of the father is noble and well drawn, also that of Lucrezia, but that of Jacopo is weak and has little theatrical effect: from the beginning I'd give him a more energetic character."

The collaboration between Verdi and Piave went ahead briskly, and by the late summer of 1844 the opera was finished. On October 3, Verdi set off for Rome to attend the rehearsals, and on November 3

Right: Scene from *I Due Foscari* in the 1988 La Scala production. Direction, sets, and costumes by Pier Luigi Pizzi.

Far right, inset: *Lord Byron in Albanian Dress*, 1835, by Thomas Phillips, National Gallery, London.

I Due Foscari was premiered. It enjoyed only modest success, and the next day Verdi wrote, "If *I Due Foscari* was not a complete failure, it was nearly so. Perhaps because the singers were very out of tune . . . the fact is, the opera was a half fiasco." He continued, "I had a great fondness for this opera: perhaps I was fooling myself, but before changing my mind I want another opinion." A few years later, in a letter to Piave dated July 22, 1848, Verdi returned to the subject, writing that the opera had "a tint, a color too uniform from beginning to end."

But even Byron's drama, to which Verdi had told Piave he should "remain attached," had been dramatically monotonous. Verdi had tried again for fast-paced theatrical action with the "positions" of the characters and the situations rendered clearly. *I Due Foscari* achieved this end, with Verdi fitting the entire story into the space of a little more than 100 minutes. One is immediately struck by the use of musical themes that aptly characterize the three principals and the Council of Ten. The musical frame has considerable impact, but inside, the dramatic situation is almost static for the entire opera, as are the attitudes of the lead characters.

I Due Foscari contains the germ of a

BYRON AND VERDI

Works by the British Romantic poet George Gordon Byron (1788–1824) inspired several musical creations. The composers who drew on Byron include Giovanni Pacini, who, like Verdi, based an opera on The Corsair *(Il Corsaro, 1813), and Gaetano Donizetti, whose* Parisina *and* Marino Faliero *were based on plays by Byron from 1815 and 1820. There is then Verdi's* I Due Foscari, *based on* The Two Foscari *of 1821.*

Byron was among the first authors to change the popular image of Venice. In place of the usual image composed of picturesque carnivals, balls, regattas, and amorous encounters, he saw a dark side of political plots and vendettas with the rigid, omnipotent, and repressive Council of Ten.

Based on an historical event drawn from the Histoire de la république de Venise *by Daru,* The Two Foscari *was written in blank verse and was in no sense suitable for theatrical use. Verdi grasped Byron's intimate poetic sensibility and managed to enrich it, avoiding certain affectations while presenting the dark atmosphere that looms over the drama. He was, however, unable to escape the story's more or less total motionlessness.*

The Corsair, a minor work by Byron published in 1814, was fun to read if not particularly appealing; it has fascinating descriptions of the Aegean. Even so, the figure of its hero, Conrad (transformed into Corrado by Piave), is memorable, a typical Byronic figure, a nonconformist adventure lover, but at the same time introverted, much like Karl von Moor of Schiller's Die Räuber, *another subject Verdi set to music (as* I Masnadieri).

theme that was dear to Verdi and that was to find full maturation in *Don Carlos*: the conflict between the demands of the state and those of the heart, of emotions. Doge Francesco is prisoner to a political system, represented by the Council of Ten, that is stronger than he is; much the same is Philip II of *Don Carlos*, who is made impotent by the excessive power of the Catholic Church.

CHARACTERS

Carlo (Charles) VII, king of France (*tenor*)
Giovanna (Joan of Arc), Giacomo's daughter (*soprano*)
Giacomo, shepherd of Domrémy (*baritone*)
Delil, an officer of the king (*tenor*)
Talbot, supreme commander of the English (*bass*)

CHORUSES AND EXTRAS
Royal officials, people of Reims, French soldiers, English soldiers, blessed spirits, evil spirits, nobles of the realm, heralds, pages, young girls, marshals, knights and ladies, magistrates, halberdiers, guards of honor

TIME: 1429.
PLACE: France, at Domrémy, at Reims, and near Rouen.

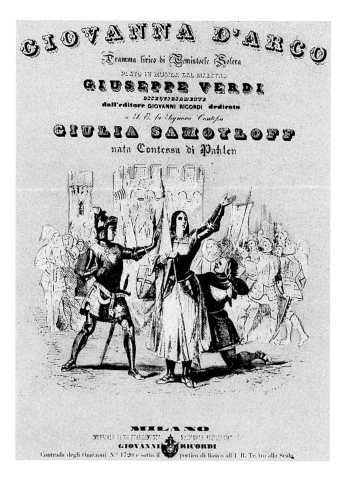

PLOT

Prologue

Great hall in the castle of Domrémy. Charles VII, exhausted by the long war against England, announces his intention to surrender to the enemy and to abdicate; he then decides to go into the nearby forest and there, in front of an image of the Virgin, to pray for the salvation of his homeland.

The scene changes to the forest. As night falls, Joan, a humble shepherdess, timidly approaches an image of the Virgin; while she is praying she becomes aware that she has been chosen for a mission, to battle the English and in that way free France. The girl's invocation achieves the desired result.

When she awakens from a mysterious sleep she finds the sovereign beside her. With words of incitement, as though inspired by an otherworldly power, she convinces him to take up his weapons, asserting that she is ready to be his guide in the struggle against the oppressors. Conquered by the young girl's ardor, Charles vows to follow her; Giacomo, Joan's father, expresses opposition in vain.

Act I

English camp not far from Reims. Under Joan's leadership, the French have won a decisive battle, and doubts and discouragement spread among the invaders. Giacomo, almost raving, expresses to Talbot his desire to enlist in the English army to fight the French so as to punish his daughter, who he thinks has betrayed him.

Gardens of the royal palace of Reims. Joan senses that her mission is nearing its conclusion and longs nostalgically for her father, wishing she could return to be with him and live in the places of her childhood. Charles intervenes, declaring his love and imploring her not to abandon him. Joan is troubled: she fears divine punishment if she dares to abandon herself to earthly love, but at the same time cannot reject his feelings. Dignitaries arrive to accompany Charles to the cathedral where the victory will be celebrated. Joan agrees to follow Charles into the church where he will be crowned victor.

Act II

A square in Reims in front of the cathedral of St. Denis. In celebration, the people welcome Charles and Joan, preceded by heralds and high officials. While the crowd disperses Giacomo appears. He has decided to come to Reims to publicly accuse his daughter. Joan reappears in the square followed by the king and the people; while Charles affirms solemnly that the country is indebted to her, Giacomo steps out of the crowd and accuses the king of blasphemy, and he then accuses his daughter of sacrilege and witchcraft. Joan, dumbfounded, bursts into tears and throws herself into the arms of her father, who demands that she be purified of her sins.

Act III

Interior of a fortress. In the course of a battle, Joan has been captured by the English and now awaits judgment. Not far away, the battle continues to rage. The chained Joan encourages her companions to fight and prays to God to free her and bring her back to lead the French troops. Giacomo, appearing, overhears her words and becomes convinced that she has been chosen by God to save her homeland from danger. He approaches her and, begging for her forgiveness, frees her from the chains. Joan takes her father's sword and rushes out to help her comrades. Her presence inspires the French to victory. The king exults, but soon afterward he receives word that the girl has been mortally wounded in the battle. Amid general sorrow, Joan, in superhuman joy and clutching to herself the French flag, dies, while all those present kneel before her body.

Opposite, top: Portrait of the soprano Teresa Stolz, Museo Teatrale della Scala. Verdi chose Stolz to play the role of Joan in a revival of the opera at La Scala in 1865. The Bohemian soprano became the ideal interpreter for many important works by Verdi, including *Don Carlos*, *La Forza del Destino*, *Aida*, and the *Requiem*.

Opposite, bottom: Title page of a period edition of *Giovanna d'Arco*, with a dedication to Countess Giulia Samoyloff.

Left: *Joan of Arc at Reims at the Coronation of Charles VII*, painting by Jules Eugène Lenepveu, 1886–90, Panthéon, Paris.

BACKGROUND AND ANALYSIS

Toward the end of November 1844, Verdi departed Rome en route to Milan. Busy with a new production of *I Lombardi* scheduled to open the season at La Scala on December 26, he was at the same time composing a new opera for the Milan theater, for which he had summoned the librettist Temistocle Solera. After Hugo and Byron, Verdi had finally turned to Schiller, who would become one of the principal sources of his libretti, including four works, *Giovanna d'Arco, I Masnadieri, Luisa Miller,* and *Don Carlos.*

Schiller wrote *Die Jungfrau von Orléans* (*The Maid of Orléans*) in 1803 and considered it to be a celebration of

Right: Joan and Charles in the opera's prologue. Performing here are the soprano Katia Ricciarelli and the tenor Flaviano Labò. Teatro La Fenice, Venice, 1972.

Below, inset: Silhouette of the German writer Friedrich Schiller by the contemporary Hank.

SCHILLER AND VERDI

Introduced to Schiller (1759–1805) by poet and translator Andrea Maffei, Verdi was fascinated by the poetic nature of Schiller's plays, with their "reality" completely detached from historical context. In Die Jungfrau von Orléans (1811), Joan of Arc dies theatrically in battle. The Romantic libertarian aspects that emerge from Schiller's text and that attracted the young Verdi were not perceived by the librettist Solera, who reduced the action of Giovanna d'Arco to a wholly ordinary story concentrated on the figures of Giovanna, her father, and the king; only a thin trace of Schiller's drama remains. Nor did things go better with I Masnadieri (based on Die Räuber [The Robbers] of 1781–82), a large-scale work in which everyone philosophizes about

everything. The play had been fascinating, but such was not true of Maffei's libretto. If not for certain musical leaps by Verdi, even the personalities of the characters, such as the manic-depressive Karl (Carlo), would have amounted to little. Kabale und Liebe (Intrigue and Love) of 1784 became Luisa Miller (1859) on a libretto by Salvatore Cammarano. In this case too the libretto represents a drastic metamorphosis. What Schiller presents as action with a complex plot is trimmed down to a simple series of scenes and musical "numbers" within a simple structure enriched by choruses. Even in Don Carlo Schiller permitted himself a great deal of historical license, and the characters often seem completely detached from historical reality.

sacrifice in the name of a supernatural calling. In reality, it ranks among Schiller's poorest dramatic texts, redundant and unorganized, but also glaringly heedless of historical realities. On the basis of this already confusing text, Solera created a libretto that, although amply trimmed of situations and characters, succeeds in being even more incongruous than its source. In Schiller's play, Joan of Arc falls in love with an English knight, creating an internal conflict between earthly love and divine mission; in Solera's libretto, Joan falls in love with the king of France. The story thus becomes even more improbable, and only Verdi's music manages to redeem, at least partially, the absurd libretto.

After having to concentrate on the gloomy story of Doge Foscari, Verdi hoped *Giovanna d'Arco* would transport him into one of those fantasy-historical paintings crowded with exciting characters and settings. In this opera he doesn't skimp on effects: marches, processions, offstage choruses, and voices and spirits, both malign and angelic, with complicated stereophonic effects. There is no lack of inspired music, alongside music that is purely decorative. Verdi manages to make the characters credible. Carlo (Charles VII), with his torments and sense of impotence, is a sort of sketch of what would become another Carlo, in *Don Carlo*. The figure of Joan is even more finely drawn. Her singing moves from moments of pure abandon to soaring, whirling cabalettas, perfectly matching her visionary character and mystical exaltation. We also meet a father figure, Giacomo, whose sad, severe singing contrasts with his daughter's. Once again Verdi presents a fundamental theme of his work: the difficult relationship between father and child.

When it premiered on February 15, 1845, the opera received a warm reception from the public, but not so much from critics, though their opinions were divided; even today the judgments on *Giovanna d'Arco* are conflicting. This work, among other things, also marked the end of the idyll between Verdi and the impresario Merelli. Irritated by Merelli's

despotic administration—freely manipulating the operas at La Scala, even inverting the order of acts II and III of *I Due Foscari*—Verdi no longer gave the Milan theater the first performance of his works. Twenty-five years would pass before Verdi decided to again present a work at La Scala.

Above: The conquest of the city of Orléans in a painting by Jules Eugène Lenepveu, Panthéon, Paris.

Left: The duet between Joan and Charles in Act I of the 1972 Venetian production. Conducted by Carlo Franci, direction by Alberto Fassini.

Alzira

Tragedia lirica in a prologue and two acts
to a libretto by Salvatore Cammarano, based
on the play *Alzire, ou Les Américains* by Voltaire

FIRST PERFORMANCE
TEATRO SAN CARLO, NAPLES, AUGUST 12, 1845

FIRST PERFORMERS
EUGENIA TADOLINI (ALZIRA), MARIA SALVETTI (ZUMA),
GAETANO FRASCHINI (ZAMORO), FILIPPO COLETTI (GUSMANO),
MARCO ARATI (ALVARO), DOMENICO CECI (OVANDO),
MICHELE BENEDETTI (ATALIBA), FRANCESCO ROSSI (OTUMBO)

CHARACTERS

Alvaro, Gusmano's father (*bass*)

Gusmano, governor of Peru (*baritone*)

Ovando, Spanish duke (*tenor*)

Zamoro, tribal chief (*tenor*)

Ataliba, tribal chief (*bass*)

Alzira, his daughter (*soprano*)

Zuma, Alzira's maid (*mezzo-soprano*)

Otumbo, Inca warrior (*tenor*)

CHORUSES AND EXTRAS
Spanish officials and soldiers, Americans of both sexes

TIME: Around the middle of the 16th century.
PLACE: Lima and other areas of Peru.

Right, top: The legendary founder of the Incas, Manco Cápac, and his companion, Mama Ocllo, from *The First New Chronicle and Good Government*, ca. 1615, written by the Peruvian Felipe Guamán Poma de Ayala. The work is an illustrated chronicle covering much of Inca history up until the arrival of the Spanish.

Right, center: The tenor Emil Ivanov in the role of Zamoro, in a scene from *Alzira* in the 1990 production at the Teatro Regio of Parma. Conducted by Gustav Kuhn; direction, sets, and costumes by Luciano Damiani.

PLOT

Prologue—The Prisoner

A vast plain at dawn, near the banks of the Rimac River. Alvaro, the Spanish governor of Peru, has been captured by a group of Inca warriors led by Otumbo. Threatened with death, Alvaro is saved by the chief of the tribe, Zamoro. With a magnanimous gesture Zamoro frees the prisoner and bids him return among his people and report that his life was saved by an Inca. As Alvaro leaves, escorted by several warriors, Zamoro learns that his betrothed, Alzira, and her father, Ataliba, are prisoners of the Spanish. He gathers his warriors and sets off to free the prisoners.

Act I—A Life for a Life

A public square in Lima. In front of the people and the highest dignitaries of the city, Alvaro relinquishes the office of governor of Peru in favor of his son Gusmano, who declares he wants peace with the Incas. To seal this pact he will marry Alzira, daughter of Ataliba.

The scene moves to the Ataliba's apartments in the governor's palace. Alzira is sleeping, watched over by her maid Zuma. The girl suddenly awakens and tells Zuma she dreamed of her beloved Zamoro, who she believes has died in battle. Ataliba enters and tries to convince his daughter to marry Gusmano; Alzira responds that she would sooner die than betray the memory of Zamoro. Meanwhile Zamoro has entered the palace and presents himself to the amazed Alzira, who has again been left alone. Their joy is of brief duration, for the two lovers are surprised by Gusmano. The governor, seeing before him one of his archenemies and realizing that the same person is also his rival in love, forgets his peace pact, calls the guard, and orders that Zamoro be cast into prison. At this moment Alvaro intervenes. Having recognized Zamoro as the man who saved his life, he asks pardon for the prisoner. Gusmano is adamant, however, and he is soon informed that the Incas have crossed the Rimac River and are threatening Lima. Zamoro is freed, not out of clemency, but only so that he can be killed in battle.

Act II–Vengeance

The Spanish fortifications around Lima. While the Spanish soldiers celebrate their victory over the Incas, prisoners are led in. Among them is Zamoro, condemned to be burned at the stake. Alzira asks Gusmano to pardon him. Gusmano agrees to do so on condition that she marry him. Overcoming her own feelings, she agrees. Zamoro is freed and with his warriors takes shelter in a cave not far from Lima, where he receives news that Alzira will soon marry Gusmano. Cursing the infidelity of his woman and swearing vengeance, Zamoro once again rushes off toward Lima.

In a room of the governor's palace, everything is ready for the celebration of the wedding. Just as the ceremony is about to begin, Zamoro, disguised as a Spaniard, approaches the groom and stabs him, then allowing himself to be imprisoned. This time Gusmano, unexpectedly, proves himself magnanimous. He pardons the murderer and gives back his beloved Alzira, then after a farewell to his father he dies.

Above: Statuette in silver of an alpaca, an animal of fundamental importance to Andean peoples.

Left: The bass Enrico Turco as Ataliba in *Alzira* at the Teatro Regio of Parma, 1990.

operas by Gaetano Donizetti: *Lucia di Lammermoor, Roberto Devereux*, and *Maria di Rohan*. The composition of *Alzira* did not begin under ideal circumstances. Verdi had a physical collapse and several disturbances emerged of a type we would today call psychosomatic: headaches and strong stomach pains. He very clearly needed rest and with difficulty managed to get the San Carlo to agree to a delay in staging the opera. As soon as he felt better, Verdi had to make up for the lost time, and the composition proceeded somewhat hurriedly. Perhaps intimidated by Cammarano's authority, Verdi did not use the domineering tones he adopted with Piave, did not impose his will as a dramatist on the librettist, and accepted the libretto somewhat passively. Voltaire's prolix and somewhat unpleasant tragedy, an Enlightenment celebration of the morality of the "good savage" in contrast to the morality that is born of Christianity, was certainly not of great interest to Verdi, and even if the work done by Cammarano to reduce the size could hardly be called drastic, the final result was revealed to be somewhat modest. Also weak was the success of the first performance: public and critics alike treated *Alzira* somewhat coldly. Similar lack of success was to inexorably mark the route of this opera.

Is *Alzira* really an ugly opera? With the conciseness that was his own, making use of hardly more than an hour and a half and employing somewhat weak characters, Verdi managed to create several moments of notable theatrical pathos. There are such excellent pieces as Alzira's cavatina "Da Gusman, su fragil barca" ("I was fleeing from Gusman in a fragile boat") in Act I and the finale of that act. In Act II there are the duet between Alzira and Gusmano and the finale of the opera.

Above: Inca warriors dragging Alvaro in the prologue of *Alzira*, Teatro Regio, Parma, 1990.

Below: Silhouette of the French philosopher and writer François-Marie Arouet, known as Voltaire, whose play inspired Verdi's *Alzira*.

BACKGROUND AND ANALYSIS

Four months after the first presentation of *Giovanna d'Arco*, a new contract had been prepared for our composer by the Teatro San Carlo of Naples, a new stage for him to conquer. The subject was drawn from *Alzire* by Voltaire and the writing of the libretto was entrusted to Salvatore Cammarano, one of the most authoritative librettists then active, the author of several of the most important

Alzira, Verdi emphasizes the contrast between the Spanish soldiers celebrating victory and the sorrowful group of Inca prisoners. We can dare suggest that we are seeing a first experiment of what would become, in *Aida*'s grandiose triumphal scene, the contrast between the triumphant Egyptians and the crowd of mournful Ethiopian prisoners.

It is a peculiarity of Verdi to stand in defense of oppressed people of any race, and he did not miss opportunities to express disapproval for every colonial act. Thus he called the English in India "sons of dogs" and expressed equal contempt for Italians in Africa: "They say

Left: The Neapolitan librettist and playwright Salvatore Cammarano, author of numerous libretti.

Below: The baritone Giancarlo Pasquetto, standing center, as Gusmano in *Alzira* at the Teatro Regio of Parma, 1990.

If we wish to construct a sort of dramatic progression that would unite Verdi's theatrical route, in *Alzira* we again encounter a theme dear to him, that of oppressed people, already presented in *Nabucco*. At the beginning of Act II of we are going there to bring civilization to those people. A fine civilization, ours, with all the miseries it carries with it. Those people don't know what to do with it, and moreover in many ways they are more civilized than we are!"

Attila

Dramma lirico in a prologue and three acts to
a libretto by Temistocle Solera, based on the play
Attila, König der Hunnen by Zacharias Werner

FIRST PERFORMANCE
TEATRO LA FENICE, VENICE, MARCH 17, 1846

FIRST PERFORMERS
SOPHIE LOEWE (ODABELLA), CARLO GUASCO (FORESTO),
NATALE COSTANTINI (EZIO), IGNAZIO MARINI (ATTILA),
ETTORE PROFILI (ULDINO), GIUSEPPE ROMANELLI (LEONE)

CHARACTERS

Attila, king of the Huns (*bass*)
Ezio, a Roman general
(*baritone*)
Odabella, daughter of the
lord of Aquileia (*soprano*)
Foresto, a knight of Aquileia
(*tenor*)
Uldino, a young Breton,
slave of Attila (*tenor*)
Leone, an old Roman (*bass*)

CHORUSES AND EXTRAS
Commanders, kings, and
soldiers of the Huns, Gepids,
Ostrogoths, Heruls,
Thuringians, and Quadi;
Druids; priestesses;
populace; men and women
of Aquileia; maidens of
Aquileia; Roman officers and
soldiers; virgins and children
of Rome; hermits and slaves

TIME: Middle of the 5th
century (AD 454).
PLACE: Aquileia and the
Adriatic lagoon (Prologue)
and near Rome (Acts I–III).

PLOT

Prologue

Aquileia has fallen into the hands of the Huns led by Attila. The prisoners being paraded in front of him include several women who have fought alongside their men; among them is Odabella. Attila is impressed by her courage and gives her his sword. Odabella vows to avenge her father with the sword of the oppressor. Ezio is introduced and in place of an honorable peace offers Attila a division of spoils. The western empire is led by the young and inexperienced Valentinian III; if the Huns and Romans unite, they can conquer and divide the domains. Ezio will have Italy, the Hun king the remainder of the two empires. Attila, certain of his power, refuses. Rome will soon be his. Ezio, in response, prepares to give battle.

The scene changes to the Adriatic lagoon where survivors, led by Foresto, arrive in search of a new homeland. The young man, still longing for his beloved Odabella, promises the exiles that a new city will arise in this lagoon.

Act I

A wood near Attila's camp. Night. Odabella mourns Foresto and the other beloved people she has lost. But he is alive and has reached the encampment. Now he stands before her, but believing her a traitor, he rejects her. She defends herself, saying she will save her homeland by killing the enemy, like the biblical Judith: "On the field of glory, I will renew the story of Judith, Odabella swears to the Lord."

Attila, asleep in his tent, is disturbed by a bad dream: before the walls of Rome a mysterious old man prevents him from touching the sacred ground. Shaking off that moment of weakness, Attila calls on his men to assemble and depart for Rome. The trumpets sound, but a religious hymn can be heard in the distance. A procession of maidens advances from the hill, followed by young men and pilgrims preceded by Leone (a stand-in for Pope Leo). Attila is petrified: it is the old man from his dream, speaking the same words. Amid general amazement the king falls to his knees before the old man.

Act II

Camp of the Roman army outside the gates of Rome. The emperor Valentinian, having concluded a peace with the Huns, has ordered Ezio to return to Rome. The general reflects bitterly on Rome's decline. Attila's emissaries arrive and invite Ezio to a banquet that will seal the peace. He accepts. Among the emissaries is Foresto, who reveals that Attila is about to be killed and urges the general to attack the enemy camp during the feast.

Everything is ready for the great banquet. Attila receives Ezio and drives off several priests who warn him of imminent danger (confirming the pervasive gloomy atmosphere, a sudden gust of wind throws the camp into darkness). Foresto takes advantage of the darkness to approach Odabella and inform her that Uldino, having joined their cause, has poured poison in the king's cup. But she doesn't want that to happen; she has vowed to take revenge herself, so when Attila is about to toast she informs him of the poison. Attila asks the name of the culprit and Foresto proudly takes responsibility. The king condemns him to death, but Odabella intervenes: she has saved the king, it should be up to her to punish the guilty one. Attila consents and, pleased by this further proof of the fierceness of this girl, announces that tomorrow she will become his bride. Turning to Ezio, he declares an end to all truces.

Act III

Woods between the camps of Attila and of Ezio. The Romans are ready to pounce on their enemies as they prepare for the wedding of Attila and Odabella. While Foresto thinks sorrowfully of his beloved's treason, she flees the Hun camp. After trying to explain her behavior, she renews her relationship with Foresto. Ezio has witnessed this scene and brings the lovers to their senses: it's time to bring the battle to an end. Suddenly Attila appears, searching for Odabella. Finding her among traitors, he realizes he has been the victim of a plot, but now it is too late. As cries of victory come from the Roman camp, Odabella stabs Attila to death.

Opposite, bottom: *Judith with the Head of Holofernes,* by Sandro Botticelli, 1470, Galleria degli Uffizi, Florence.

Above: Samuel Ramey as Attila in the 1991 La Scala production, conducted by Riccardo Muti.

Below: Attila halted at the gates of Rome. Teatro La Fenice, Venice, 1986.

BACKGROUND AND ANALYSIS

Following the Neapolitan failure of *Alzira*, in August 1845 Verdi returned to Milan. The weight of work and a decidedly low morale led him to the brink of another psychophysical collapse. His commitments were becoming only more pressing, and Verdi, aside from taking into consideration several interesting offers that arrived from Paris and London, had to fulfill his obligation with the Teatro La Fenice in Venice. He pulled out of a drawer the play *Attila* by Zacharias Werner, which he had looked at during the time of *I Due Foscari*. It was a good story for the Venetian opera house, and Verdi laid the groundwork by sending the librettist Piave his own draft of the libretto, with the so-called positions indicated.

Werner (1768–1823) had been a late Romantic writer of no great interest. He can be remembered, and only in the negative sense, for having been among the asserters of the "racial" superiority of the German people over the Latin cultures. Verdi certainly paid no heed to these aspects, although they are clear enough in Werner's *Attila*, in particular his contempt for the Italic peoples, looked upon as traitors and cowards, poisoners and intriguers. Even in Verdi's opera, the characters of Ezio and Foresto are by no means paragons of loyalty and are clearly contrasted to the figure of Attila, a warrior who has a barbarous nature but at the same time shows great nobility and a fearlessly combative spirit. Verdi, however, places a female figure on the same level as the Hun—the warlike, proud, and most of all Italic Odabella. In this way the composer not only presents a vital figure but adds the theme of rebirth, inserting a scene that has no source in Werner, that being the founding of Venice in the prologue.

Verdi had already begun work on the new score when he suddenly changed his mind and decided the unfortunate Piave was not a suitable librettist for this subject and moved the work to Solera. Working with Solera was no easy thing: lazy and perennially undecided, he had to be constantly urged forward. Verdi's stress got only worse as the date of the opera's premiere approached, and early in January he ended up in bed, struck down by a serious form of gastric fever. In the end the opera was performed at La Fenice on March 17, 1846, to great success. Not surprisingly, the scene of the founding of Venice was particularly pleasing to the audience. Equally delighted was the public's reaction to the phrase Ezio directed at Attila: "You can have the universe / But leave Italy to

me." To which the Venetians called out, "To us! Italy to us!" It is astonishing that this powerfully allusive phrase somehow made it past the Austrian censors!

Despite the enthusiasm with which Verdi approached the composition, the final result, perhaps in part because of his state of health, is somewhat uneven, even though the score contains areas of excellent composition. We can cite, for example, the storm that opens the scene of the lagoon in the prologue and the later dawn with the chorus of pilgrims in the foreground with the response from the distant refugees, on the sea. This is a moment of enormous theatrical effectiveness. Also ranking as truly great is the encounter between Attila and Leone in Act I. The terrorized Attila expresses himself with short, declaimed phrases; the strings depict the superstitious fear to which he is victim; we will encounter them again, years later, in the "Mors stupebit" of the *Requiem*.

TEMISTOCLE SOLERA

Adventurer and nonconformist, Temistocle Solera (1815–1878) was Verdi's "political" librettist, as Francesco Maria Piave was his "middle-class" librettist. With a father who had died in Spielberg prison, and being often at the center of conspiracies and escapades himself, Solera was the poet best suited for transmitting patriotic ideals. His libretti, from Nabucco *to* I Lombardi *and* Giovanna d'Arco, *contain clear references to the political situation of the time. The libretto of* I Lombardi *is far from a poetic and theatrical masterpiece but is saved by the "current" aspects of its subject: the people of Milan, who a*

few months earlier had identified with the Hebrews of Nabucco, *now donned the helmets and armor of the Lombard Crusaders to free a Jerusalem that was a stand-in for Milan. The historical boundaries of the libretto fell away: so when the Lombards sang, "Today the Holy Land will be ours," the audience responded, "Yes!" In* Giovanna d'Arco *Solera moved away from Schiller, transforming the story into something from a feuilleton, but not without a certain verve. Verdi saw Solera as a "lazybones librettist" but entrusted him with* Attila. *Solera delivered the work to Verdi, but when Verdi wanted changes, Solera had left for Madrid. It was thus Piave who reworked* Attila, *marking the end of Verdi's collaboration with Solera. After further events that saw Solera an impresario in Spain, a secret agent of Napoleon III and Cavour, and even an antiquarian in Paris, he ended his days sadly and in poverty, dying in Milan in 1878.*

Macbeth

Melodramma in four acts to a libretto
by Francesco Maria Piave, based on the
tragedy by William Shakespeare

FIRST PERFORMANCE
TEATRO DELLA PERGOLA, FLORENCE, MARCH 14, 1847

FIRST PERFORMERS
MARIANNA BARBIERI-NINI (LADY MACBETH), FELICE VARESI (MACBETH),
NICOLA BENEDETTI (BANCO), ANGELO BRUNACCI (MACDUFF)

FIRST PERFORMANCE OF THE REVISED VERSION
THÉÂTRE LYRIQUE, PARIS, APRIL 21, 1865
AMÉLIE REY-BALLA (LADY MACBETH), ISMAËL (MACBETH),
JULES BILIS-PETIT (BANCO), JULES-SÉBASTIEN MONJAUZE (MACDUFF)

CHARACTERS

Duncano (Duncan), king of Scotland (*silent*)
Macbeth, a general in Duncan's army (*baritone*)
Banco (Banquo), a general in Duncan's army (*bass*)
Lady Macbeth, Macbeth's wife (*soprano*)
Lady-in-waiting to Lady Macbeth (*mezzo-soprano*)
Macduff, a Scottish nobleman, thane of Fife (*tenor*)
Malcolm, Duncan's son (*tenor*)
Fleanzio (Fleance), Banquo's son (*silent*)
A servant of Macbeth (*bass*)
A doctor (*bass*)
A murderer (*bass*)
A herald (*bass*)

APPARITIONS
The ghost of Banquo

CHORUSES AND EXTRAS
Witches, messengers of the king, Scottish nobles and refugees, murderers, English soldiers, aerial spirits

TIME: 1040.
PLACE: Scotland, principally Macbeth's castle. Act IV begins on the border between Scotland and England.

Top: Title page of one of the first editions of the score of *Macbeth*.

Right: *Lady Macbeth Seizing the Daggers*, by Henry Fuseli, exhibited 1812, Tate Gallery, London. Macbeth, trembling, extends the bloody daggers, and Lady Macbeth, without hesitation, rushes to grab them from him.

PLOT

Act I

On a desolate Scottish heath, Macbeth and Banquo, victorious soldiers, encounter a group of witches. Amazed, they listen to the witches' predictions: Macbeth will be named thane of Cawdor and will take the throne of Scotland; Banquo, although he himself will not become king, will have royal descendants. Their amazement is transformed into consternation when several soldiers announce that the thane of Cawdor, accused of treason, has been executed and that the title will now go to Macbeth.

The scene changes to Macbeth's castle. Lady Macbeth sees the prophecies of the witches and their rapid fulfillment a clear sign of destiny. The visit of King Duncan presents the opportunity to carry out a monstrous plan: kill the ruler in his sleep and seize

the crown of Scotland. At first Macbeth hesitates, but then he carries out the murder, and Lady Macbeth smears the king's sleeping servants so they will be accused of the crime. It is dawn. Macduff

arrives, a noble in the entourage of the king, together with Banquo. Macduff enters the royal rooms to awaken the king and immediately returns, horrified. The courtiers come running at his calls, along with Macbeth and his wife. Banquo announces that Duncan has been murdered.

Act II

Macbeth is king of Scotland, and Malcolm, Duncan's son, has fled to England, fueling the suspicion that he was behind his father's murder. Even so, Macbeth does not feel secure: the witches promised the crown to the descendants of Banquo, who thus must

chair. In vain the woman tries to restore peace among the guests, while her husband, terrorized, raves in disconnected phrases. With difficulty Macbeth manages to control himself and decides to once again interrogate the witches.

Act III

A dark cave. The witches reassure Macbeth: his power is not in danger. The spirits, although warning him to beware of Macduff, guarantee him that no one born of woman can defeat him and that his power will endure as long as Birnam Wood does not march against him.

Still not satisfied, Macbeth wants to know if the descendants of Banquo will

The soprano Maria Callas, historic interpreter of Lady Macbeth, in the first important revival of Verdi's opera, at La Scala, in 1952.

die, along with his son Fleance. The ambush is successful, but only in part: Banquo is mortally wounded, but Fleance manages to flee.

A sumptuous banquet is going on in the royal castle, and Lady Macbeth offers welcome to her guests. Suddenly the atmosphere changes: Macbeth sees the ghost of Banquo seated on the royal

reign. The witches do not want to respond; forced to do so by Macbeth, they show him eight kings, the last holding a mirror in which the earlier ones are reflected over and over. Deeply disturbed, Macbeth faints; when he comes to, he is beside his wife. Following her instigation he decides to exterminate Macduff and all his family.

The baritone Renato Bruson, one of the greatest interpreters of the role of Macbeth, in a production of the opera at the Teatro San Carlo in Naples, 1984–85 season. Conducted by Riccardo Muti, directed by Sandro Sequi, sets and costumes by Giacomo Manzù.

VERDI AND MACBETH

Verdi's love for Shakespeare, and for Macbeth in particular, bordered on the maniacal. Beginning with his attention to the writing of the libretto, he overlooked nothing in his effort to make the best musical setting of the tragedy. In Giuseppe Verdi, Il Genio e Le Opere (1887), Eugenio Checchi reports several statements from Marianna Barbieri-Nini, the first Lady Macbeth. "The rehearsals," she said, "both piano and orchestra, came to more than one hundred. Verdi, implacable, did not care if he wearied the artists and tormented them for hours on end with the same piece. And until the interpretation was attained that seemed closest to the ideal in his mind, he did not proceed to the next scene. He was not much loved by those who worked for him, for not a word of encouragement ever left his lips.

Never a 'bravo' of conviction, not even when the orchestra or choir believed they had done their utmost to please him." Barbieri-Nini also spoke about how Verdi, as a highly attentive director, continued to advise on the stage action: "The sleepwalking scene took me three months of study: for three months, morning and night, I sought to imitate those who speak while sleeping, articulating words (as Verdi told me) almost without moving their lips, and leaving the rest of their faces immobile, including the eyes. It drove me crazy . . . As for the duet with the baritone that begins, 'Fatal mia donna, un murmure' ['My fatal woman, a murmur'], you may think I'm exaggerating, but it was rehearsed more than a hundred and fifty times so it might be closer to 'speech' than 'singing.'"

Inset, above: A portrait of William Shakespeare.

Opposite, bottom: The great concertato that closes Act I, in the famous La Scala production of 1975, with principals Shirley Verrett and Piero Cappuccilli. Conducted by Claudio Abbado, directed by Giorgio Strehler, sets and costumes by Luciano Damiani.

Opposite, top: Costume for Lady Macbeth, designed by Luigi Bartezago for the La Scala, Milan, production during the 1873–74 season.

Act IV

Macduff and Malcolm are camped on the border of Scotland, ready to give battle to the usurper. Malcolm orders his soldiers to cut branches from the trees in the nearby Birnam Wood and carry them in their attack. Meanwhile, in the royal castle, Lady Macbeth is suffering insane nightmares and relives the crimes committed beside her husband. This is the moment of the end for the murderous couple: Macbeth, abandoned by everyone, senses the approach of the final battle. The announcement that Birnam Wood is moving freezes him, and he rushes into the battle. Macduff appears in front of him; by now about to succumb, Macbeth yells that no one born of a woman can kill him. Macduff responds that he was extracted by force from the belly of his mother. The predictions have all come true; Macbeth is lost. Mortally wounded, he curses the crown for which he has been cursed, while Duncan's son Malcolm is acclaimed king of Scotland.

BACKGROUND AND ANALYSIS

For Verdi the moment had come to pause. After *Attila* his psychophysical state was truly at the limit; he was supposed to leave for London, where he was awaited for an undertaking at Her Majesty's Theatre, but his doctor prohibited him from going.

For six months Verdi did absolutely nothing, assisted by his faithful Emanuele Muzio, his only student, but also his helper, factotum, and collaborator who was always at his side. Through major crises and signs of recovery, Verdi made it to the autumn of 1846. It was then that he again made contact with the theatrical world. Still not feeling well enough to take on London, he decided to sign a contract with Alessandro Lanari, impresario of the Teatro della Pergola in Florence.

He thus began work on *Macbeth*, a task to which he immediately gave special attention, not overlooking a single detail: nothing was to escape his control. He himself wrote a detailed dramatization of the text, which he then sent to Francesco Maria Piave: "Here is the draft of *Macbeth*. This tragedy is one of the greatest creations of man.... If we can't make something great out of it, let us at least try to do something out of the ordinary. The draft is clear: unconventional, simple, and short. ... There must not be a single useless word: everything must say something." The libretto, on which Andrea Maffei was called to assist,

Above: The baritone Piero Cappuccilli (Macbeth) and the soprano Olivia Stapp (Lady Macbeth) in a 1986 production at the Teatro La Fenice, Venice. Conducted by Gabriele Ferro, direction by Luca Ronconi, sets and costumes by Luciano Damiani.

Below: Conductor Claudio Abbado, whose interpretation of Verdi's *Macbeth* is tied to the revival of that opera.

was constantly checked and revised to achieve almost total adherence to Shakespeare's text. For his part, the composer supervised the cast of performers, followed their preparations, and even gave indications for the scenery and the costumes.

Thus *Macbeth* represents an almost unique case in the career of Verdi, aware as he was that the work represented a fundamental step in his movement as a dramatist toward what he defined as "the theatrical word" ("la parola scenica") or the intention to "invent the truth." In this work Verdi

also emerges as a great orchestrator: every coloristic detail of the instruments coincides perfectly with the theatrical situation.

The opera was performed to great success on March 14, 1847, and was repeated over the following years in numerous theaters in Italy and the rest of Europe; on the occasion of its first performance in Paris, in 1865, Verdi undertook various modifications.

Macbeth in the 1865 Revised Version
Eighteen years after *Macbeth*'s premiere, in Florence in 1847, the French

publisher Léon Escudier proposed that Verdi make a French version. For this occasion Verdi reused the score, which even years later he thought very important, introducing only a few cuts and integrations. In Act I Verdi added the "S'allontanarono" ("They have gone") chorus of the witches after Macbeth and Banquo depart. He thus changed the twenty-four beats in the presto that ends the duet between Lady Macbeth and Macbeth, beginning with "Oh, potessi il mio delitto dalla mente cancellar" ("Oh, if I could erase the crime from my mind!"). Act II opened with a new aria for Lady Macbeth, "La luce langue" ("The light is fading"), a splendid work of great theatrical force that notably enriches her character. This aria replaced the cabaletta "Trionfai! Secure alfine!" ("Triumph! Secure at last"). There were then some retouchings, mostly technical, in the banquet scene. Act III was notably different from the 1847 version. Completely new was the ballet, obligatory for the Paris Opéra. The witches' chorus that opens the act was also reworked, as was the later scene of the kings' apparitions. The act ended with a duet between Lady Macbeth and Macbeth, "Ora di morte e di vendetta" ("Hour of death and vengeance"), that replaced a vigorous and perhaps undervalued—possibly even by Verdi—cabaletta for Macbeth, "Vada in fiamme, e in polve cada" ("Go up in flames, and fall into dust"). The "Patria oppressa" ("Oppressed homeland") chorus that opens Act IV was completely reworked for Paris. There is then the final scene of the battle, for which Verdi reworked the orchestration. "You'll laugh," he wrote a friend, "when you see that I've written a fugue! I, who detest everything that smacks of theory! But I assure you that in this case the fugue is permissible. The mad chase of subjects and counter-subjects, and the clash of dissonances, and the general uproar can suggest a battle quite well." A monologue that saw Macbeth die on stage was suppressed in this version and replaced by a large choral work, a hymn to victory, not completely convincing but even so the source of an enthusiastic finale.

The Parisian version, which is the one performed most often today, was greeted at its premiere as a great success by the public, while critics called attention to certain incongruities: some even accused Verdi of not knowing Shakespeare. This provoked his indig-

nant response: "I may not have rendered *Macbeth* well, but that I do not understand and feel Shakespeare, no, by God, no! He is one of my preferred poets, and I have had him in my hands from my earliest youth, and I read and reread him continually!" A few years later, in a more meditative moment, Verdi had to admit, "All things considered, *Macbeth* is dull. Amen."

An exaggerated conclusion that cancels nothing of the uniqueness of this opera.

Set design sketch by Girolamo Magnani for Act II of *Macbeth*, Teatro alla Scala, 1873–74 season.

I Masnadieri

Melodramma in four acts to a libretto
by Andrea Maffei, based on the play
Die Räuber by Friedrich Schiller

FIRST PERFORMANCE
HER MAJESTY'S THEATRE, LONDON, JULY 22, 1847

FIRST PERFORMERS
JENNY LIND (AMALIA), ITALO GARDONI (CARLO),
FILIPPO COLETTI (FRANCESCO), LUIGI LABLACHE (MASSIMILIANO),
LEONE CORELLI (ARMINIO), LUCIEN BOUCHÉ (MOSER)

CHARACTERS

Massimiliano, Count
Moor (*bass*)
Carlo, his son (*tenor*)
Francesco, Carlo's brother
(*baritone*)
Amalia, orphaned niece
of Massimiliano (*soprano*)
Arminio, the count's
chamberlain (*tenor*)
Moser, a pastor (*bass*)
Rolla, robber companion
of Carlo (*tenor*)

CHORUSES AND EXTRAS
Wayward youths (robbers),
women, children, servants

TIME: Early 18th century,
spanning about three years.
PLACE: Germany.

PLOT

Act I

A tavern on the border of Saxony. Carlo Moor has abandoned his paternal home to join up with other idle youths. Weary of this dissipated life, he has written to his father, imploring pardon. He hopes to return home and again see his beloved cousin Amalia. The reply he receives dashes all hopes; his brother, Francesco, writing in their father's name, forbids him to return home. Carlo's reaction is immediate: he and his friends decide to become bandits, with Carlo as their leader.

The scene shifts to the castle of the counts of Moor in Franconia. Francesco, who hates his brother, makes clear his perfidy: he has destroyed the letter Carlo sent their father and now, determined to take possession of everything, gives the coup de grâce to the old count. Assisted by his niece Amalia, the ailing Massimiliano receives his servant Arminio, disguised and bearing false news: the much-loved firstborn Carlo has died in

battle. The proof is a blood-stained sword and a message in which he asks his father to have Amalia marry his brother, Francesco. Amalia is desperate and Massimiliano, undone by sorrow, falls to the floor, apparently dead.

Act II

Francesco, new count of Moor, celebrates his new state with a splendid banquet. Amalia, meanwhile, weeps at Massimiliano's tomb. She is joined by Arminio, who reveals to her that Carlo and the count are still alive. Amalia is happy and, after again sharply rejecting the offers of love from Francesco, flees from the castle.

The scene shifts to a forest in Bohemia, not far from Prague, where the robbers have set up camp. Carlo has been storming through the city to liberate Rolla, his right-hand man. While all exalt the courage of the robber, Carlo senses that the road he has taken is without return and thinks with sorrow of his beloved Amalia. His companions call him back to reality: the forest has been surrounded.

Act III

An open space not far from the forest surrounding Massimiliano's castle. Amalia, who has taken refuge in the forest, is terrified to hear the voices of robbers. She begs for mercy from the first man she encounters, but her anguish turns to joy when she realizes it is Carlo. She then tells him the fate of his father and the evil deeds of Francesco, and he proclaims his love. He cannot find the courage to admit he is the leader of the robbers and suffers great anguish.

The scene moves to the forest, by the ruins of an old tower. It is night. The robbers are asleep as Carlo contemplates suicide, while a shadow moves toward the tower: Arminio. Carlo follows him and blocks the way. The man reveals that

hidden in the tower is the old Moor, whom he has saved from the prison where he was thrown by Francesco, who intended he should die of hunger.

Horrified by this revelation, Carlo awakens the robbers and makes them

vow to bring him Francesco, wherever he is to be found.

Act IV

Rooms in the castle of Massimiliano. Francesco awakens terrified from a dream in which he witnessed his damnation. The pastor Moser sternly reminds him of the seriousness of sins like parricide and fratricide. Francesco angrily asks him for absolution, and the pastor responds that only God can give him that. In the distance, meanwhile, the calls of the robbers can be heard as they are about to storm the castle.

It is dawn in the forest. Undone by his situation, the old Massimiliano bewails the death of his favorite son, Carlo, although Carlo stands beside him, unrecognized. Carlo asks for him for a blessing.

The robbers arrive: the castle has been wiped out and they have captured Amalia; Francesco, however, has fled. At this point Carlo is forced to reveal his true identity: he is the leader of this gang of cutthroats. Amalia and Massimiliano are astonished by this discovery, but Amalia declares herself ready to love him all the same, preferring death to being abandoned again. Carlo does not want her to live with him in dishonor and stabs her, then flees to surrender himself to justice.

Above: The second scene in Act II of the opera in a production at the Teatro Municipale of Piacenza, 1998. Conducted by Carlo Franci, direction by Beppe De Tomasi, sets by Giuseppe Ranchetti, costumes by Pier Luciano Cavallotti.

Opposite and left: Two lithographs of *I Masnadieri* published in the periodical *L'Italia Musicale*, 1849.

BACKGROUND AND ANALYSIS

Before beginning the composition of *Macbeth*, Verdi sent his friend Maffei a libretto in prose based on *Die Räuber*, Schiller's first play. *I Masnadieri* (*The Robbers*) was initially supposed to be an opera for Florence, but Verdi later decided to write *Macbeth*. He'd already begun drafting the score of *I Masnadieri* during the autumn of 1846, but he now put it aside.

After *Macbeth*, Verdi was again in touch with Benjamin Lumley, impresario of Her Majesty's Theatre in London. So it was that *I Masnadieri* was settled upon to be the work that would introduce Verdi to the London public. On his return to Milan, Verdi quickly set about composing the opera, while back in London Lumley, using great skill, paved the way for the new work to be greeted as a real social event, one that would go down in the annals of the theatrical life of the British capital.

At the end of May 1846, Verdi set off for London, preceded by the faithful Muzio. Verdi stopped in Paris to greet his old friend Giuseppina Strepponi. Having retired from the stage, the singer had moved to the French capital, where she kept busy giving singing lessons. The romantic relationship between Verdi and the former prima donna is usually said to have begun with this "Parisian stopover." Verdi arrived in London, and although "the climate was

Inset: *Countess Clara Maffei*, portrait by Francesco Hayez, ca. 1845. Wife of Andrea Maffei, the countess was also a friend of Verdi's.

Below: The final scene of Act I of *I Masnadieri* at the Teatro Municipale of Piacenza, 1998. The photo shows the soprano Fiorenza Cedolins (Amalia), the bass Giorgio Giuseppini (Massimiliano, on the floor), and the baritone Giovanni Meoni (Francesco).

horrendous to me," and in fact caused him more than a few physical and emotional disturbances—the composer was already showing signs of hypochondria—he set to work with great concentration and determination. The premiere took place on July 22, 1847, the day on which the British Parliament went on vacation. Queen Victoria and Prince Albert were present at the theater, along with all of the House of Lords, the duke of Wellington, and Prince Louis Bonaparte, among many others. The success was tremendous, thanks in part to its cast, standing out among them the soprano Jenny Lind in the role of Amalia.

The opera's success did not, however, have a positive effect on its destiny. In fact, *I Masnadieri*, along with other Verdian operas from these early years, was soon dropped from the repertoire. Why? In his memoirs, *Reminiscences of the Opera*, Lumley suggested one possible reason: "The libretto was even worse constructed than is usually the case with adaptations of foreign dramas to the purpose of Italian opera." Once again the libretto was one of the most clearly negative aspects of the opera. *Die Räuber* was Schiller's first play and is long and prolix; in order to be faithful to the original, Maffei had adopted a pretentious style crammed with moralistic pronouncements, which in Schiller have a certain logic, but which in a

libretto become heavy and useless. Perhaps out of respect for Maffei, Verdi did not intervene, as he usually did, to have things his way, and the result often borders on the ridiculous.

Without doubt, Verdi was fascinated by the torments of Carlo Moor, who turns robber out of the love for justice, and his opposite, Francesco, a figure of evil without hope. The composer, however, delved no deeper than the surface, and *I Masnadieri* almost seems like an opera about circumstances, a product well produced to suit the singers, in

particular Lind, and the public. The orchestration is careful, while the characterizations of the figures in the libretto are certainly of little help, although the figure of Francesco reveals certain features that would later reappear in the Iago of *Otello*.

Verdi conducted the first two performances and then passed the remainder to the Briton Michael Balfe, returning to his life in Italy, not without stopping in Paris along the way. On July 27, 1847, Verdi and Muzio were in Paris again. Muzio soon left for Milan, while Verdi remained in the French capital to work out several arrangements with the Opéra (which would lead to the performance of *Jérusalem*) and naturally to again visit Strepponi.

Left: The soprano Ilva Ligabue (Amalia) and the bass Boris Christoff (Massimiliano) in Act I of *I Masnadieri* at the Teatro dell'Opera, Rome, in 1972. Other performers in this important revival were the tenor Gianni Raimondi and the baritone Renato Bruson. Conducted by Gianandrea Gavazzeni.

Above: The tenor Nunzio Todisco as Carlo in a production of *I Masnadieri* at the Teatro dell'Opera in Pisa.

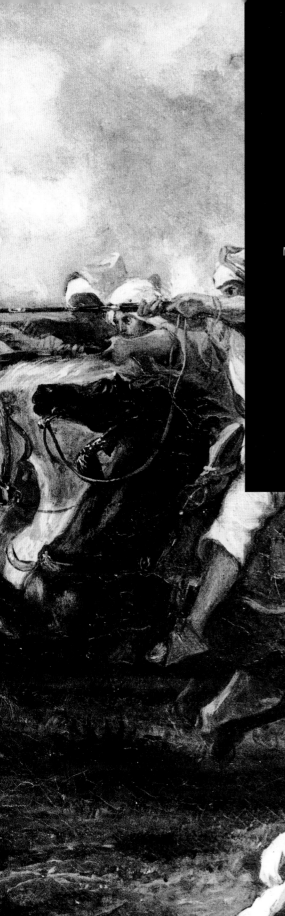

Il Corsaro

Melodramma in three acts to a libretto
by Francesco Maria Piave, based on
Lord Byron's poem *The Corsair*

FIRST PERFORMANCE
TEATRO GRANDE, TRIESTE, OCTOBER 25, 1848

FIRST PERFORMERS
MARIANNA BARBIERI-NINI (GULNARA), CAROLINA RAPAZZINI (MEDORA),
GAETANO FRASCHINI (CORRADO), ACHILLE DE BASSINI (SEID),
GIOVANNI VOLPINI (GIOVANNI), GIOVANNI PETROVICH (SELIMO)

Corrado, captain of the corsairs (*tenor*)
Giovanni, a corsair (*bass*)
Medora, Corrado's young lover (*soprano*)
Gulnara, Seid's favorite slave (*soprano*)
Seid, pasha of Coron (*baritone*)
Selimo, official of the pasha (*tenor*)
A black eunuch (*tenor*)
A slave (*tenor*)
Anselmo, a corsair (*silent*)

CHORUSES AND EXTRAS
Corsairs, odalisques, soldiers, eunuchs, Muslims, slaves, Turks, handmaidens of Medora

TIME: Early 19th century.
PLACE: An island in the Aegean and the Turkish city of Coron.

PLOT

Act I

The island of the corsairs in the Aegean. While a group of corsairs exalts the free life, their captain Corrado meditates on his life as an outlaw, a choice he made and cannot now flee. His lieutenant, Giovanni, enters with a letter; Corrado reads it rapidly and then gives his men the order to prepare to set sail. He will take command of an expedition against the Muslims.

The scene changes to Medora's rooms in an old tower. Medora, Corrado's betrothed, suffers constantly over the fate of her beloved. He arrives, but only to tell her that he is again about to set sail. Medora tries in vain to hold him back, fearing she will never see him again, but a cannon sounds from the bay and Corrado departs.

Act II

In the Turkish city of Coron. In a splendid room of the harem of the pasha Seid. Gulnara, Seid's favorite, expresses her hatred for the sultan and hopes to regain her freedom. One of Seid's eunuchs enters and invites Gulnara to take part in the feast to celebrate the coming victory over the corsairs. Gulnara accepts.

In a magnificent pavilion near the port of Coron. Amid ongoing festivities, a slave introduces a poor dervish, just escaped from the corsairs. The man responds evasively to the questions Seid puts to him. Suddenly a blinding light fills the space: the sultan's fleet is on fire. The dervish throws off his disguise: it is Corrado! The other corsairs rush in, as the Turks flee. The battle rages, and there are flames everywhere. With great generosity, Corrado does what he can to save the women of the harem, among them Gulnara, saved by Corrado himself. He, however, is captured by the Turks. Seid condemns him to death. In vain Gulnara asks for clemency.

Right: A scene from Act II of *Il Corsaro* at La Fenice in Venice, 1971. Conducted by Carlo Franci, direction by Alberto Fassini, sets and costumes by Pier Luigi Pizzi.

Opposite, left: The soprano Katia Ricciarelli, shown here in *Roberto Devereux* by Gaetano Donizetti, won RAI's "Voci Verdiane" competition in 1971, performing Medora's aria from Act I of *Il Corsaro*, a role she played the next year at the Teatro Verdi in Trieste.

Act III

In the rooms of the sultan in the fortress. Seid, suffering jealousy, fears Gulnara has become infatuated with the corsair who saved her from the flames. He summons her and during their conversation has confirmation of his suspicions: she loves Corrado. Seid leaves, furious, but not before threatening Gulnara, who, in turn, is more determined than ever to get revenge.

The scene changes to the tower of the fortress. Corrado lies in chains. Gulnara enters. He saved her life and she loves him and is now ready to help him escape. But Corrado refuses: his sense of honor prevents him. Gulnara grabs a dagger and rushes out only to return shortly, her face pale: she has killed Seid. At this point Corrado agrees to flee, if only to save the woman from a terrible punishment.

The scene returns to the island of the

Below: The year 1848 saw revolutions all over Europe. This period illustration shows the "mobile trenches" of bundled sticks designed by Antonio Carnevali and the painter Borgocarati used by the combatants in Porta Tosa, Milan, a "true battle that went on through the fifth day."

corsairs. Medora, surrounded by her maidens, is near the end of her life. With her are also the corsairs who have escaped from the attack on Coron. Medora has lost all hope: Corrado is dead, her life has no more purpose. Suddenly a sail appears on the horizon: Corrado! Followed by Gulnara, the corsair has the time to embrace his beloved, who dies in this arms. The desperate Corrado then throws himself from the tower while Gulnara falls to the ground in a faint.

Right and below: Two other scenes from the 1971 production of *Il Corsaro* at La Fenice. The performers include Giorgio Casellato Lamberti (Corrado), the sopranos Vasso Papantoniou (Medora) and Angeles Gulin (Gulnara), and the baritone Renato Bruson (Seid).

BACKGROUND AND ANALYSIS

Understanding the birth of *Il Corsaro* requires returning to 1845, when Verdi was working on *Giovanna d'Arco*. After that work's La Scala premiere, a somewhat malicious review appeared in the *Gazzetta Musicale di Milano*, published by Ricordi. This made Verdi angry with Giovanni Ricordi, who was also his publisher, and out of spite he signed a contract for three operas with Francesco Lucca, Casa Ricordi's direct rival. The first was destined for Her Majesty's Theatre in London, and negotiations began. Verdi thought the most fit subject for the London theater was Byron's *The Corsair*

and entrusted the libretto to Piave. The publisher Lucca had a very different opinion, but Verdi responded decisively: "I'm doing *Il Corsaro* or nothing." Thus, amid spite and stubbornness—destined to bring the Verdi-Lucca collaboration to a rapid end—*Alzira* was staged in Naples and *Attila* in Venice. Verdi, despite the psychophysical collapse he suffered after the Venice premiere, continued to defend his intention to do *Il Corsaro*. When Piave, to meet another commitment, asked for his libretto back, Verdi wrote to him, "What's this? Have you become crazy or are you about to become so! Give you back *Il Corsaro*, that *Corsaro* which has always fascinated me and which I've thought about so much, and which you've versified with more care than usual?"

Meanwhile, Verdi finished *Macbeth* (Florence, 1847), and when the London commitment came up, the idea of *Il Corsaro* no longer appealed to him so much, his attention by then drawn to *I Masnadieri*, based on Schiller. In July 1847 *I Masnadieri* opened in London, after which Verdi dedicated himself to *Jérusalem*, the reworking of *I Lombardi* for France, which premiered at the Opéra of Paris on November 26, 1847.

At that point *Il Corsaro* reappeared. While still in Paris, Verdi returned to its composition, but in an almost distracted way and working somewhat hurriedly; the subject and Piave's libretto no longer satisfied him, but Verdi put little effort into making changes. Having finished the opera, he sent the score to Lucca with a terse note: "Upon the payment of 1,200 gold napoleons of twenty francs that Sig. Lucca will be pleased to make in Milan to Sig. Emanuele Muzio, the above-named Lucca will become absolute proprietor of the libretto and score of *Il Corsaro* that I have expressly composed to fill the obligation I had with him by contract signed October 16, 1845." From then on, for Verdi *Il Corsaro* was finished business. With the excuse of a bad cold, plus the 1848 uprising in Paris and Strepponi's presence there, Verdi did not budge from France. So *Il Corsaro* was entrusted to Emanuele Muzio, who directed its October 25, 1848, premiere at Trieste's Teatro Grande. The cast was first-rate: Marianna Barbieri-Nini, Gaetano Fraschini, and Achille De Bassini, all voices especially loved by Verdi. But they could not save the work from the hostility of the Trieste public, perhaps offended by Verdi's failure to attend.

Il Corsaro did not fall into oblivion as speedily as had poor *Alzira*, but clearly Verdi did very little to encourage further performances. He had written the score in a hurry, perhaps, but it was not contemptible. The two women are well formed, most of all vocally: Medora's singing is purely lyrical, Gulnara's more markedly dramatic. Corrado and Seid stand out among the men, and in them we can see traits that would become the passionate ardor of Manrico and the vindictive jealousy of the Count di Luna of *Il Trovatore*. There are also musical sections of value, beginning with the beautiful bel canto inflections of the Act I scene and romance of Medora, "Non so le tetre immagini" ("I don't know how to dispel these dark thoughts"), perhaps the opera's most famous piece. Also notable is Gulnara's Act II cavatina, "Vola talor dal carcere" ("Sometimes my thoughts fly from prison"); and interesting for its dramatic writing is the duet of Gulnara and Seid in Act III. Also in that act is the notable prison scene and the opera's finale, with the trio of Medora, Corrado, and Gulnara, which highlights the great expressivity and refinement of Verdi's instrumentation.

A lively caricature of Verdi from the Villa Verdi at Sant'Agata.

Below, inset: Francesco Maria Piave, Verdi's dedicated and patient librettist, in a portrait of the period.

FRANCESCO MARIA PIAVE

Between 1844 and 1862 Verdi's closest and most faithful literary collaborator was Francesco Maria Piave (1810–1876). His encounter with Verdi at La Fenice—where he was official poet, stage manager, and resident director, responsible for all visual aspects of operas—led to Ernani *(1844). That same year Verdi asked him to write* I Due Foscari. *In 1846 it was* Attila; *although Verdi had inexplicably turned to Solera for this work, he fell back on the always-available Piave to make changes to the libretto. Verdi and Piave then worked together on* Macbeth *(1847).*

Piave's later work with Verdi included Il Corsaro *(1848),* Stiffelio *(1850), and that work's later conversion into* Aroldo *(1857). He also worked on two of Verdi's "popular trilogy,"* Rigoletto *(1851) and* La Traviata *(1853). In 1857 there was the tormented writing of* Simon Boccanegra. *Their final collaboration was* La Forza del Destino *(1863).*

Those seeking the main reason behind this collaboration have always emphasized Piave's availability and his submissiveness to Verdi's tyrannical demands. Doubtless aware of his artistic inferiority, Piave kept his comments to a simple, "The Maestro wants it so, and that's enough!" In 1859 he moved to La Scala, where he assumed the same positions he'd occupied at La Fenice, librettist and stage manager. A serious, paralyzing illness forced him to abandon the theater in 1867. Reduced to poverty, he was supported only by Verdi, who also paid the expenses of his funeral.

La Battaglia di Legnano

Tragedia lirica in four acts to a libretto
by Salvatore Cammarano, based on the play
La Bataille de Toulouse by Joseph Méry

FIRST PERFORMANCE
TEATRO ARGENTINA, ROME, JANUARY 27, 1849

FIRST PERFORMERS
TERESA DE GIULI-BORSI (LIDA), VINCENZA MARCHESI (IMELDA),
GAETANO FRASCHINI (ARRIGO), FILIPPO COLINI (ROLANDO),
PIETRO SOTTOVIA (BARBAROSSA), LODOVICO BUTIA (MARCOVALDO)

CHARACTERS

Federico Barbarossa,
German emperor (*bass*)
First consul of Milan (*bass*)
Second consul of Milan
(*bass*)
Mayor of Como (*bass*)
Rolando, Milanese leader
(*baritone*)
Lida, Rolando's wife
(*soprano*)
Arrigo, Veronese warrior
(*tenor*)
Marcovaldo, a German
prisoner (*baritone*)
Imelda, Lida's servant
(*mezzo-soprano*)
A herald (*tenor*)

CHORUSES AND EXTRAS
Knights of Death;
magistrates and dukes of
Como; handmaidens of Lida;
Milanese people; Milanese
senators; warriors of Verona,
Brescia, Novara, Piacenza,
and Milan; German army

TIME: 1176.
PLACE: Milan (Acts I, III,
and IV) and Como (Act II).

Above, inset: Portrait of
Frederick I Hohenstaufen,
called Barbarossa (1122–
1190). Museo del Castello,
Milan.

Right: Lida and her hand-
maidens in Act I of
the opera (to the right, the
soprano Fiorenza Cedolins
in the role of Lida), Teatro
Regio, Parma, 1999.
Conducted by Patrick
Fournillier, direction by
Flavio Ambrosini, sets and
costumes by Carlo Savi.

PLOT

Act I—He Is Alive!

Milan. The people welcome with great joy the soldiers of the Lombard League. Among them is the young Arrigo, believed by many to have died in battle. Rolando, his brotherly friend, joyfully embraces him and leads him to his home.

Rolando's castle. Lida, Rolando's wife, is upset by sad thoughts: she has lost all her family and also Arrigo, the man she loved before marrying Rolando. She is overcome by emotion when she sees Arrigo with her husband. When Rolando is called away by the Milanese senate, Arrigo tells Lida she is faithless. She replies that everyone thought he was dead and that her dying father forced her to marry Rolando. Arrigo rejects her and, in despair, hurries off.

Act II—Barbarossa

In the town hall of Como, a city allied with Barbarossa. Arrigo and Rolando try to convince the citizens to side with Milan. The leader of the council reminds them that they are joined to Barbarossa by a pact, to which Arrigo and Rolando respond with contempt. Suddenly Barbarossa appears, and he violently rejects the Milanese ambassadors, confirming his intention to destroy hostile cities. War cries are heard.

Act III—Infamy

Milan, crypt of Sant'Ambrogio. The Knights of Death, who have pledged to die rather than suffer defeat, have assembled and have welcomed Arrigo as a member. All vow to drive the hated foreigners from the soil of Italy.

The scene returns to the castle of Rolando. Lida fears for Arrigo's life: she knows he has joined the Knights of Death, and with a letter she hopes to dissuade him from that sacrifice. She is joined by her husband, who, sensing the approach of the decisive battle, wants to take leave of his wife and son. As soon as Lida has withdrawn, Arrigo arrives. Rolando tells him that he has been chosen to lead the Knights of Death. In the event that Rolando dies, Arrigo vows to take care of his family. The emotion of Rolando contrasts with the reluctance and the emotional upheaval of Arrigo, who goes away distressed. Left alone, Rolando is approached by Marcovaldo, who has intercepted the note from Lida to Arrigo and shows it to him: it is proof that the relationship between the two has never ended. In distress, Rolando vows to get revenge.

In a room in a tower, Arrigo is preparing for battle when Lida arrives, having waited in vain for a response to

her note. The old passion seems to be rekindled, but Lida's sense of duty to her husband soon takes over. She begins to explain the contents of her note, but is interrupted by repeated knocking on the door. Lida hides on the balcony as Rolando appears in the doorway. After confronting Arrigo for not having told him he had enlisted in the Knights of Death, he goes onto the balcony and discovers his wife.

Arrigo offers his life as proof of Lida's innocence, but Rolando wants revenge and storms away, locking Arrigo in the tower. From the street below rise trumpet blasts calling the soldiers to battle. Out of desperation Arrigo leaps from the tower into the water below.

The Battle of Legnano (detail), ca. 1860, by Amos Cassioli (1832–1891). Galleria d'Arte Moderna, Florence.

Act IV—To Die for the Homeland!
A square in Milan. Lida, Imelda, and the citizens pray for victory. Their prayers mingle with the distant sounds of voices shouting victory. A consul bears a message: the imperial forces have been defeated. The people exult, but they hear the sorrowful sounds of a horn. Arrigo is brought into the square, mortally wounded. Dying, he swears to Rolando that Lida is innocent. The two friends are reconciled, and as Arrigo dies the Te Deum sounds and the standards are folded before the dead body of the hero.

BACKGROUND AND ANALYSIS

The year 1848 was a time of revolutions, and all of Europe was shaken by insurrections, Italy as much as any other country. From north to south, barricades were set up in streets in the name of liberty and the constitution. Verdi was still in Paris, where he planned to collaborate on a patriotic opera for the Italian cause.

A new contract with the Teatro San Carlo was postponed precisely because of the 1848 uprisings. For this Neapolitan venture, Verdi, in Paris, and Cammarano, in Naples, engaged in a barrage of letters in the attempt to choose a subject suitable for the situation. In the end they agreed on *La Bataille de Toulouse* by Joseph Méry, which became *La Battaglia di Legnano* (*The Battle of Legnano*). The reference to the historical battle of 1176 made clear references to the current political situation; indeed, Legnano was among the cities still occupied by the Austrians.

Compared to *Alzira*, the work of collaboration between Verdi and Cammarano led to a far more interesting result, but *La Battaglia di Legnano* was not completed until the end of 1848. Ricordi thought Rome would make the ideal site for the opera's premiere. The city was about to proclaim the Roman Republic, and on the evening of January 27, 1849, the uproar at the Teatro Argentina was uncontrollable. All of Act IV had to be encored, and not only during the premiere but also during later performances. The opera's fate, however, was tied to the political situation. So it was that in coming years, with the complete reestablishment of Austrian power in Italy, censors were anything but understanding toward such a shamelessly subversive opera. A few reworkings to disguise this aspect turned *La Battaglia di Legnano* into *L'Assedio di Arlem*, but that score fell

---

SALVATORE CAMMARANO

Born into a theatrical family—his grandfather Giancola was the greatest Pulcinella of San Carlino in Naples—Salvatore Cammarano (1801-1852) was the family "poet." His father painted, and he too was drawn to painting before turning to poetry academies, but he was drawn most of all to theater. He wrote comedies and tragedies with some success, but found his true calling in music. The "theatrical poet" was a figure in great demand in the century of Romantic melodrama. The work was hectic, with outrageous deadlines. At heart it meant taking events from original sources or novels, reducing them to the canonical three acts, and versifying them while the composer was already at work. Cammarano immediately established himself as a true "champion." With his talents it was inevitable he would become one of the most important collaborators, as well as a friend, of another master of speed, Gaetano Donizetti, for whom he wrote the libretti for *Belisario, Lucia di Lammermoor, L'Assedio di Calais, Pia de' Tolomei, Roberto Devereux, Maria de Rudenz,* and *Poliuto.*

His meeting with Verdi, on the occasion of Verdi's debut at the Teatro San Carlo in Naples, where Cammarano was official librettist, was not among the best. After a somewhat unhappy beginning with Alzira (1845), their relationship and their understanding greatly improved, as indicated by their heavy correspondence. The results were La Battaglia di Legnano (1849), Luisa Miller (1849), and Il Trovatore, which marked the end of their collaboration: Cammarano died suddenly, and Leone Emanuele Bardare had to complete the libretto.

---

into oblivion, along with almost all the others from this youthful period.

In this work too Verdi demonstrated his usual dramatic precision, his ability to never take his eye off the requirements of theatrical intensity and efficacy. *La Battaglia di Legnano* is a work of great vitality and consistent

looms the contrast between human passions, with their heavy load of weaknesses, and the heroic ideal, which rings out like something almost mystical and pure.

Verdi accentuated this need for heroism with the highly effective use of musical themes. The "Viva Italia! sacro

Opposite, top: Gianandrea Gavazzeni, conductor of the 1961 La Scala production. Performers included the tenor Franco Corelli, the soprano Antonietta Stella, and the baritone Ettore Bastianini.

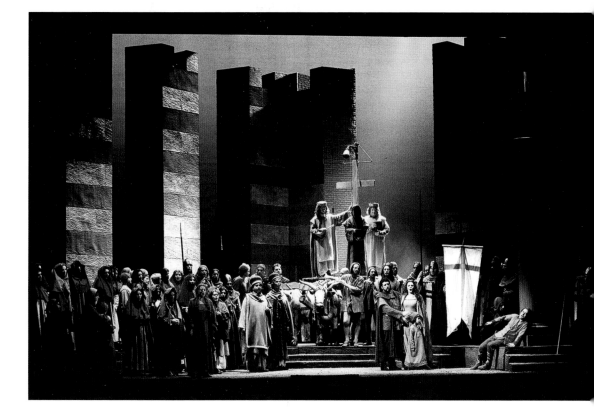

inspiration; the contrast between its public aspects, meaning the historical moment, and those that are private, meaning the amorous events of the three protagonists, is perfectly balanced. Without doubt, patriotic tints prevail, but at the same time they serve to render even more dramatic the interior conflicts of the individuals. The amorous themes, in the true sense of the term, are just touched on and are extinguished with equal speed, as indicated by the duet between Arrigo and Lida that ends Act I. Over all of this

un patto" ("Long live Italy! A sacred pact"), used in both vocal and instrumental forms, runs through the entire opera. The attention given to thematic values, the melodic coloring, and the careful use of timbre suggest a certain French influence on Verdi's style. The last act presents more than a few suggestions drawn from the magniloquent world of the "grand opéra," and certainly *La Battaglia di Legnano* presents itself as a keystone to a compositional phase that was by then already undergoing profound changes.

Opposite, inset: The librettist Salvatore Cammarano, author of more than fifty libretti, including many famous works for Donizetti and Verdi.

Above: The death of Arrigo in Act IV of the opera, at the Teatro Regio of Parma, 1999. The performers include Alberto Cupido (Arrigo), the soprano Fiorenza Cedolins (Lida), and the baritone Roberto Servile (Rolando).

Luisa Miller

Melodramma tragico in three acts to a libretto
by Salvatore Cammarano, based on the play
Kabale und Liebe by Friedrich Schiller

FIRST PERFORMANCE
TEATRO SAN CARLO, NAPLES, DECEMBER 8, 1849

FIRST PERFORMERS
MARIETTA GAZZANIGA (LUISA), MARIA SALVETTI (LAURA),
TERESA SALANDRI (FEDERICA), SETTIMIO MALVEZZI (RODOLFO), ACHILLE DE BASSINI
(MILLER), ANTONIO SELVA (WALTER), MARCO ARATI (WURM)

CHARACTERS

Count Walter (*bass*)
Rodolfo, his son (*tenor*)
Federica, duchess of
Ostheim, Walter's niece
(*mezzo-soprano*)
Wurm, Walter's steward
(*bass*)
Miller, an elderly retired
soldier (*baritone*)
Luisa, his daughter
(*soprano*)
Laura, a peasant girl
(*mezzo-soprano*)
A peasant (*tenor*)

CHORUSES AND EXTRAS
Villagers, Federica's
ladies-in-waiting, pages,
retainers, archers

TIME: First half of the
17th century.
PLACE: A village in Tyrol.

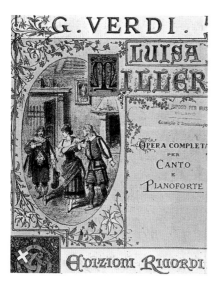

Cover of *Luisa Miller*, transcription of the complete opera for piano and voice.

PLOT

Act I—Love

It is Luisa's birthday, and the villagers have gathered to celebrate. Luisa is unable to disguise her anxiousness: her beloved Carlo has not yet arrived. When he does finally show up, dressed to go hunting, he declares his love. While everyone else heads off toward the church, Miller is taken aside by Wurm; he loves Luisa and wants Miller's permission to marry her, but Miller has no intention of forcing his daughter into marriage. The angry Wurm reveals Carlo's true identity: he is the count's son, Rodolfo. To his great distress, Miller thus learns that all his fears have been justified.

The scene changes to a hall in Walter's castle. Count Walter, having learned from Wurm that his son is infatuated with a village girl, decides to rush his son's wedding to the duchess Federica.

Rodolfo tries to oppose his father's will and, trusting that the woman will understand, confesses to her that he cannot love her since he is in love with another. Finding herself so openly rejected, Federica cannot disguise her jealousy.

Interior of the Miller home. Luisa awaits Carlo, while from a distance are heard horn blasts and the voices of hunters. It is Miller, who arrives and reveals to his daughter the deceit of which she has been a victim. Rodolfo hears the last portion of this conversation and once again proclaims his love for Luisa. Now the count arrives, having followed his son, and in menacing tones accuses Luisa of being a vulgar seductress. Miller defends his daughter, while the count calls his men and orders that the father and daughter be thrown in prison. Rodolfo opposes this injustice, but the count pays no heed. At this point the young man turns on his father and declares that if he doesn't release Luisa, Rodolfo will reveal the way the count acquired his title. Luisa is immediately freed.

Act II—Intrigue

The Miller home. Laura and other villagers inform Luisa that her father has been taken by the count's men. Luisa wants to rush to the castle, but Wurm's arrival stops her. He informs her that her father has been condemned to death for having resisted the count. There is a way, however, in which Luisa might save his life. She must only do what the count wishes her to do.

She has no choice. Following dictation, she writes a letter addressed to Wurm, in which she declares her love for him. At midnight she will be prepared to flee with him. Luisa is forced to never reveal that she was forced to write this letter.

In the castle, Wurm relates to the count the happy outcome of his mission. During this dialogue we understand that the two are accomplices in the assassination of the legitimate heir to the house of Walter. As Wurm leaves to take charge of Luisa, Federica arrives. Count Walter reassures her that Rodol-

Garden of the castle. A villager, sent by Wurm, hands Rodolfo the letter forced out of Luisa. After an initial moment of anguish, Rodolfo wants to seek revenge: he calls Wurm and challenges him to a duel. Overcome by terror, Wurm shoots in the air, drawing the attention of the count and the servants. Claiming to be ready to carry out every desire of his son, the count urges him to marry Federica to avenge the betrayal.

Act III—The Poison
The Miller home. Luisa, desperately unhappy, is writing a letter. Laura and other village women seek to encourage her, keeping her in the dark about the coming wedding of Rodolfo and Federica. Miller, freed from prison, tenderly embraces his daughter: he knows what she has suffered to save him. Luisa offers her father the letter and asks him to give it to Rodolfo. Miller understands what is

Opposite, top: A scene from Act I in a production at the Teatro Regio of Parma in 1991. Conducted by Eugene Kohn, directed by Lorenzo Mariani, sets by Luigi Marchioni, costumes by Steve Almerighi.

Below: The American soprano Kallen Esperian, who replaced Katia Ricciarelli in *Luisa Miller* at La Scala in 1989.

fo no longer gives a thought to Luisa. The girl has always loved Wurm, as she herself will confirm. Brought before Federica, Luisa, aware that her father's life hangs in the balance, repeats the lies she has been forced to accept.

in that letter: Luisa, after having explained the intrigue, proposes to Rodolfo a suicide pact. Miller, desperate, begs his daughter to live. Distraught, Luisa tears the paper and agrees to leave with her father the next morning. Miller

Above: The finale of Act I of *Luisa Miller* at the Teatro alla Scala in 1989. This production was marked by the public's reaction against the soprano Katia Ricciarelli.

The German poet Friedrich Schiller. His plays inspired composers such as Verdi, Rossini, Mercadante, Donizetti, Pacini, and others.

The façade of the Teatro San Carlo in Naples, in an engraving from the mid-19th century.

BACKGROUND AND ANALYSIS

Verdi returned to Paris a few days after the opening of *La Battaglia di Legnano*. From there he witnessed the sequence of events, with the repression of the nascent republics. Early in August he continued on his way to Italy and Busseto, where he was soon joined by Strepponi. His financial situation had greatly improved, he could easily permit himself a certain ease, and he could choose a lifestyle at a certain level: the choice fell on the Dordoni palace, today Palazzo Orlandi.

He was working with Cammarano to fulfill the contract with the San Carlo in Naples, the one postposed by the 1848 uprisings. In terms of the choice of subject, Verdi had in mind an historical romance, *L'Assedio di Firenze*, by Domenico Guerrazzi, but the ferocious repression going on in Naples made that seem a highly unlikely choice. Cammarano wrote to Verdi: "I can't do any better than turn to a subject you once proposed, Schiller's *Kabale und Liebe*."

Having chosen the subject, the librettist took the situation in hand and made the necessary cuts and changes. The five original acts were reduced to three. Fearing the censors, Cammarano lowered the social level of the characters: the prime minister became a more anonymous count; his son changed names from Ferdinand—the name of the king—to Rodolfo. With the libretto rearranged, the work proceeded briskly: at the end of October *Kabale und Liebe* (*Intrigue and Love*), transformed into *Luisa Miller*, was finished. Verdi set off for Naples, a city he had never gotten along well with, going back to the days of *Alzira*. The relationship did not improve with *Luisa Miller*, so Verdi decided not to compose anything more for that city—a promise that in fact he

goes off. Unseen, Rodolfo enters, pours a vial of poison into a pitcher of water and then, with firm resolve, turns to Luisa. He shows her the letter to Wurm and Luisa admits writing it. Rodolfo asks for something to drink. He drinks and offers Luisa the glass so she can taste the bitter liquid. She too drinks. Rodolfo, in anger, takes her to task for her infidelity and reveals that the two of them have just drunk poison. Almost with joy, finally freed of her

terrible oath, Luisa tells the truth to the increasingly desperate Rodolfo. Miller returns to find the two youths dying. The count and Wurm also arrive, and as Luisa dies, Rodolfo stabs Wurm to death.

kept. *Luisa Miller* premiered on December 8, 1849, and met with success that was not, however, free of clouds.

Much has been said about the opera's "middle-class" aspects or about the definitive change in Verdi's style said to have begun with this opera. What should be emphasized instead is that Verdi always proceeded with great consistency and lucidity. Even those works that can be considered his weakest do not lack traces of his progress toward this dramatic-theatrical ideal. This ideal does indeed appear

Dark, almost claustrophobic tones prevail, and it's no accident that most of the action (with the exception of two scenes) takes place indoors, contrasting the Miller home with the Walter castle, a contrast that emphasizes the differences, and not only social, between the two families. Once again Verdi presents us with the theme of parents versus children. Two fathers, Miller and Count Walter, with very different motivations and visions, want the best for their children. The old soldier wants joy and

more clearly in this opera, beginning with the dramatic color of the instrumentation, which quite purposefully seems to want to give the setting a sort of "local" atmosphere; Verdi thus employed a Germanic type of instrumentation, beginning as early as the sinfonia, in which the clarinet emerges and impresses a fundamental color on the entire opera.

respectability for Luisa; for the count, instead, what is good for Rodolfo is measured only by way of wealth and social standing. Verdi gives all of these characters a passionate force; beside the pride of the two fathers is the passionate and dramatic ingenuousness of the two young lovers. Amidst all of this there is evil: Wurm.

The concertato in Act I of *Luisa Miller* at the Teatro Regio of Parma, in 1991. From left to right, the bass Enrico Turco (Count Walter), the tenor Alberto Cupido (Rodolfo), the soprano Alessandra Pacetti (Luisa), and the baritone Giancarlo Pasquetto (Miller).

Stiffelio

Melodramma in three acts to a libretto by
Francesco Maria Piave, based on the play *Le Pasteur*
by Émile Souvestre and Eugène Bourgeois

FIRST PERFORMANCE
TEATRO GRANDE, TRIESTE, NOVEMBER 16, 1850

FIRST PERFORMERS
MARIETTA GAZZANIGA (LINA), GAETANO FRASCHINI (STIFFELIO),
FILIPPO COLINI (STANKAR), RANIERI DEI (RAFFAELE), FRANCESCO REDUZZI (JORG)

Stiffelio, an Ahasuerian
preacher (*tenor*)
Lina, his wife, daughter
of Stankar (*soprano*)
Stankar, an old colonel,
count of the empire
(*baritone*)
Jorg, an elderly
preacher (*bass*)
Raffaele, a nobleman
of Leuthold (*tenor*)
Federico di Frengel,
Lina's cousin (*tenor*)
Dorotea, Lina's cousin
(*mezzo-soprano*)
Fritz, servant (*silent*)

CHORUSES AND EXTRAS
The count's friends,
Stiffelio's disciples,
Ahasuerians

TIME: Early 19th century.
PLACE: Germany, in and
around Stankar's castle
on the Salzbach River.

PLOT

Act I

A hall in Count Stankar's castle. Friends and relatives of the Protestant minister Stiffelio, also Stankar's son-in-law, have gathered in the castle to await his return from a mission. During the wait the elderly minister Jorg reads to them from *Der Messias* (*The Messiah*), the epic poem by Klopstock. Everyone is happy when Stiffelio returns, followed by Lina, his wife, and several friends, among them Raffaele, Lina's lover.

Stiffelio recounts how the castle's boatman told him a strange story about seeing a man and woman leave the castle at dawn by way of a window, letting fall a packet of letters along the way; in fact, the boatman has given the letters to Stiffelio. At hearing this news Lina and Raffaele give a start. Stiffelio understands that the letters have to do with an

extramarital affair, and in a magnanimous gesture he tosses the packets into the fire. Left alone with Lina, Stiffelio sees how upset she is and is struck to see that she is not wearing her wedding ring. He asks for an explanation, but Stankar interrupts him: the guests are waiting for him. Lina decides she must confess her adultery. Stankar returns silently and, watching her, understands what has happened. In a dramatic conversation he imposes silence on her: the truth would be a mortal blow to Stiffelio and it would also dishonor the family. When Lina and Stankar leave the scene, Raffaele enters. Unaware that he is being observed by Jorg, he hides a letter to Lina in the *Messias*, then closes the metal clasp on the volume. Both Lina and Jorg have keys to the volume. At this point Lina's cousin Federico arrives and takes the volume. Jorg, who has observed the scene, is convinced that Federico is the seducer and soon reveals his conviction to Stiffelio. Stiffelio grabs the volume out of Federico's hands. The note falls out, but is quickly grabbed by Stankar, who then tears it in pieces. Stiffelio is furious with his father-in-law, who secretly challenges Raffaele to a duel.

Act II

A cemetery near the church. While Lina prays at her mother's tomb, she is joined by Raffaele. Lina rejects him and asks him to give back her ring, otherwise she will reveal everything to Stiffelio. Their conversation is interrupted by Stankar, who orders his daughter to go away, then gives a sword to Raffaele for their duel. Stiffelio arrives, interrupting the duel and tries to reconcile the two challengers. At this point Stankar reveals that Raffaele is the traitor. Stiffelio, upset, asks Lina to prove her innocence. She says nothing. Stiffelio, furious, grabs a sword and rushes at

Raffaele, but the distant voices of his faithful followers intoning a hymn of penitence stop him. Jorg appears on the threshold of the church, calling Stiffelio to his duties as pastor. Overcome by emotion, Stiffelio collapses.

Act III

A hall in Stankar's castle. Raffaele has fled the area, but not without first asking Lina to come join him. Stankar, seeing himself dishonored, decides to kill himself. Jorg arrives with the news that Raffaele, recalled by Stiffelio, has returned to the castle. Stiffelio enters, followed by Raffaele. Stiffelio asks the incredulous Raffaele if he'd like to marry Lina, but says that first he himself must have a final conversation with her. He asks Raffaele to go into a nearby room so he can hear what is said. In cold tones Stiffelio reminds Lina that their marriage is not valid because they got married when he was living under a false name to escape persecution. He can thus present her with a divorce decree. Only her signature is missing. In vain Lina implores him and confesses that she loves him; in the end, driven by the harsh reproofs of her husband, she signs the decree. At that moment Stankar enters with a bloody sword: he has killed Raffaele, and the family's honor is saved. The disturbed Stiffelio allows Jorg to lead him to the church.

The congregation sings a penitential psalm, among them Stankar and Lina. The pale Stiffelio, almost tottering, climbs to the pulpit. Jorg calls on him to

Opposite: *La Corsia dei Servi*, by Giuseppe Canella, 1834. The view is down a central street in Milan.

Above: A scene from Act I of *Stiffelio*, Teatro La Fenice, Venice, 1985.

Below: The soprano Linda Roark-Strummer (Lina) and the tenor Antonio Ordonez (Stiffelio), Teatro La Fenice, Venice, 1988.

BACKGROUND AND ANALYSIS

After the first three performances of *Luisa Miller*, in December 1849, Verdi left Naples to return to Busseto. As always his mind was in continuous ferment, seeking new ideas, more than ever in search of subjects that convinced him totally. He began to elaborate new ideas in which he could involve Salvatore Cammarano. It was during this period that his attention was drawn to *Le Roi S'Amuse* by Victor Hugo, destined to become *Rigoletto*, and to *El Trovador*, the play by Antonio García Gutiérrez. Also the project for *Re Lear* returned to his mind, destined to once again end in failure.

The tenor Jesus Pinto (Aroldo) and the bass Franco Federici (Godvino) in Act III of *Aroldo*. Conducted by Eliahu Inbal; direction, sets, and costumes by Pier Luigi Pizzi. Teatro La Fenice, Venice, 1985.

find inspiration and comfort in the Bible. Stiffelio lets the book fall open and finds it has opened to the story of Christ and the woman taken in adultery. Reaching the word "forgiven," and deeply moved, he looks to Lina and makes it clear that she has his forgiveness.

AROLDO

Verdi tried everything to save Stiffelio. *After it had been transformed into* Guglielmo Wellingrode *in Rome and Naples, Verdi wrote to Ricordi, "If we really must do* [Stiffelio] *first of all the censors must be persuaded that nothing in that book is against politics or religion and permit the original libretto with all the words and the respective mise en scène. . . . It should be made without any alterations or castration and with all the dedication possible by everyone. . . . Without these conditions I cannot permit* Stiffelio *to be done."*

Stiffelio *seemed destined for oblivion, even if Verdi, referring to his operas in 1854, wrote, "Two I would not want to see forgotten are* Stiffelio *and* La Battaglia di Legnano." *So it went until 1856, when*

Verdi and Piave again took up the opera; Piave convinced Verdi to transport it to the Middle Ages and make the protagonist a crusader. Hence the birth of Aroldo, *which opened the new theater of Rimini, on August 16, 1857. It was a success, but more out of respect than genuine conviction.*

The changes Verdi made are of no great weight, the two versions matching in nearly every sense: a few changes in key or in a cabaletta, such as the one that closes the scene with Lina, the original "Perder dunque voi volete" ("Then you want to destroy"), a somewhat conventional number, changed to the far more dramatic and intense "Ah, dal sen di quella tomba" ("Ah, from the depths of that tomb"). The radical change was in the finale.

Leaving Cammarano the chore of working out the subjects, Verdi undertook a new project with Ricordi, an opera to be performed in the autumn of 1850. The publisher would find the theater, following the custom of that time. For this new opera Verdi turned to Francesco Maria Piave; knowing Verdi's fondness for new subjects, Piave suggested a French play, *Le Pasteur* (*The Pastor*), staged in Paris in February 1848 and, oddly enough (given its "thorny" subject), already circulating in an Italian translation that Piave had a copy of.

Verdi was very fond of the subject, and Piave managed to prepare a good libretto, although not always clear in the exposition of events and the precedents of the story. So began the composition of *Stiffelio*, among the most troubled in all of Verdi's production. For the first time, Verdi had chosen a subject that took place in the "contemporary" world (destined to happen only once more, with *La Traviata*); the story tells of a Protestant minister, there is adultery, there is a confession scene, and the finale is in a church with the addition of a Gospel quotation. To censors, this was pure manna. The opera, destined for the Teatro Grande in Trieste, was performed with a certain success, but it had already been purged of all religious references. Verdi strenuously defended his creation, but in the later performances in Rome and Naples the opera was completely altered: the minister Stiffelio was transformed into a German statesman named Guglielmo Wellingrode.

In the end it was Verdi himself, tired of seeing his opera reduced to a sort of blank canvas on which more or less anything could be made to happen, who decided to carry out changes that at least followed a certain logic. So it was that *Aroldo* came into being, which for Verdi was the definitive version of the opera: he even went so far as to order that the original be destroyed!

To our good fortune, *Stiffelio* was saved and has survived to this day in all its peculiar beauty and originality. It is a novelty not only in its subject but also in its use of voices and the orchestra. For the first time, Verdi gave a tenor a strong character full of contrasts, and we would have to wait for *Otello* to find another so intensely dramatic. The father figure is not absent, represented here by the ambivalent role of Stankar: a loving father, bearer of moral values, but at the

same time a cruel and vindictive man. The torments and lacerations of Lina anticipate the passions and disturbances of Amelia in *Un Ballo in Maschera*; the

Below: *View of the Piazza del Duomo with the Coperto dei Figini*, by Angelo Inganni, 1838. The reference is to the porticoed building at left.

scene in the cemetery, with the splendid aria "Ah! dagli scanni eterei" ("Ah! From the heavenly thrones"), is a precursor of the scene of the "orrido campo" ("horrid field") in *Ballo*.

Stiffelio represents an absolutely fundamental forward step in Verdi's concept of the theater of emotions and intimate conflicts, which was destined to find its highest expression in *Don Carlos*.

Opposite, right: The tenor José Carreras, aside from being the protagonist on the only official recording of *Stiffelio*, in 1980, sang the role in an important production at the Royal Opera House, Covent Garden, in 1993.

Rigoletto

Melodramma in three acts to a libretto
by Francesco Maria Piave after the play
Le Roi S'Amuse by Victor Hugo

FIRST PERFORMANCE
TEATRO LA FENICE, VENICE, MARCH 11, 1851

FIRST PERFORMERS
TERESA BRAMBILLA (GILDA), ANNETTA CASALONI (MADDALENA),
RAFFAELE MIRATE (DUKE), FELICE VARESI (RIGOLETTO),
PAOLO DAMINI (SPARAFUCILE), FELICIANO PONZ (MONTERONE)

CHARACTERS

The duke of Mantua
(*tenor*)
Rigoletto, his court jester
(*baritone*)
Gilda, Rigoletto's daughter
(*soprano*)
Sparafucile, a hired
assassin (*bass*)
Maddalena, his sister
(*contralto*)
Giovanna, Gilda's
governess (*mezzo-soprano*)
Count Monterone
(*baritone*)
Marullo, a knight
(*baritone*)
Matteo Borsa, a courtier
(*tenor*)
Count Ceprano (*bass*)
Countess Ceprano, his
wife (*mezzo-soprano*)
A court usher (*bass*)
A page of the duchess
(*mezzo-soprano*)

CHORUSES AND EXTRAS
Noblemen, ladies,
halberdiers, pages

TIME: 16th century.
PLACE: Mantua and its
environs.

Above: Scene of the quartet
in the last act of the opera
in an image from 1851.

PLOT

Act I

A room in the ducal palace in Mantua. During a ball, the duke, a fascinating youth of easy morals, tells the courtier Matteo Borsa he is infatuated with a beautiful girl he spotted in church. Meanwhile he is courting the countess of Ceprano, under the eyes of her husband, the count. Rigoletto, the court jester, hurls his usual mordant ironies at the unfortunate count, while a truly surprising piece of news circulates among the courtiers: Rigoletto has a lover. Count Ceprano proposes abducting her to get revenge for the jester's pungent comments about him.

The ball is at its peak when Count Monterone arrives. The duke has seduced his daughter, and Monterone wants justice from the duke for the offense to his daughter's honor. Rigoletto cruelly mocks Monterone, who, at the height of his outrage and before being taken away by guards, curses the jester and his lord. Rigoletto is truly frightened by the curse.

It is night in a deserted street near the house where Rigoletto lives with his daughter, beside the Ceprano palace. Still disturbed by the curse, Rigoletto makes his way home. He is followed by a

shadow—the assassin Sparafucile, who offers his services for a fee. For the moment Rigoletto refuses and sends him away. Disturbed by this encounter, Rigoletto embraces his daughter, Gilda, and reminds her to never let anyone come near her. He repeats these instructions to the governess, Giovanna, who, however, has already accepted payment to let the duke into the garden. When Rigoletto leaves, the duke throws himself at Gilda's feet, courting her ardently and pretending to be a "poor student." The captivated girl confesses that she loves him. The sound of steps in the street hurries the duke on his way.

In the street are Count Ceprano and the other courtiers who have assembled to abduct the presumed lover of Rigolet-

to. When Rigoletto returns, Marullo tells him that they are going to abduct the countess of Ceprano. Rigoletto agrees to take part in the action. Blindfolded, he holds the ladder, but soon realizes he has been tricked: Gilda has been abducted.

Act II

A room in the ducal palace. The duke returned to Gilda's house only to find her not there, and he now fears she has been abducted.

The courtiers arrive and recount to him the tale of the night's adventure and how they abducted Rigoletto's lover. The girl has been taken to court, and the duke runs to her. Rigoletto appears. Destroyed by sorrow, he examines every corner, looking around, trying in vain to find traces of his daughter, and in the face of the courtiers' mockery he reveals his secret: it is not his lover, but his daughter, they have stolen from him. Threatening and begging, in vain he asks for her to be given back. Gilda is in the duke's rooms, from which comes the sound of crying. Rigoletto drives off the courtiers and listens to his daughter's story of how she was seduced and tricked.

Suddenly the door flies open: Monterone is about to be taken to prison. Rigoletto vows vengeance for himself and for Monterone.

Playbill from the premiere of *Rigoletto* at the Teatro La Fenice, Venice, March 11, 1851.

Below: The celebrated tenor Enrico Caruso in the costume of the duke of Mantua.

Left: The baritone Michael Lewis as Rigoletto in a production at the Teatro La Fenice in Venice in 1992. Conducted by Vjekoslav Sutej, directed by Andrei Serban, sets by Gianni Quaranta, costumes by Dada Saligeri.

Act III

It is night, on the right bank of the Mincio River, where stands Sparafucile's tavern. Paid by Rigoletto, the killer has succeeded—thanks to the charms of his sister Maddalena—in attracting the duke. Rigoletto watches from outside: he has brought Gilda so she can see the unworthiness of the man she continues to love. Meanwhile the duke uses his full repertory as a skilled seducer to conquer Maddalena; not insensitive to the duke's charm, she persuades her brother to spare him, and to kill in his place the first person to come into the tavern during the night.

Gilda has heard all of this. In vain her father has arranged for her to wear men's clothing and leave immediately for Verona. Instead she knocks on the door, Sparafucile gets in place with his dagger, and Maddalena opens the door. Gilda falls under the dagger of the killer, who stuffs her body in a sack he gives to Rigoletto, who pays the rest of the agreed sum. Left alone, the jester is relishing the joy of revenge when he hears the duke singing in the distance. With terror he opens the sack and finds his dying daughter, who begs him to forgive her. Rigoletto recalls Monterone's curse and falls lifeless on his daughter's body.

Scene from Act II of *Rigoletto* with the baritone Renato Bruson (Rigoletto) and the soprano Andrea Rost (Gilda) in the 1994 La Scala production. Conducted by Riccardo Muti, directed by Gilbert Deflo, sets by Ezio Frigerio, costumes by Franca Squarciapino.

The famous duet "Sì, vendetta" ("Yes, vengeance"), which closes Act II of *Rigoletto*, performed by the baritone Leo Nucci and the soprano June Anderson. Teatro La Fenice, Venice, 1992.

BACKGROUND AND ANALYSIS

A few months after the premiere of *Stiffelio*, the directors of the Teatro La Fenice asked Verdi for a new work to inaugurate the new season. Verdi accepted and with Francesco Maria Piave got busy seeking a suitable subject. At first Verdi was drawn to a work by Alexandre Dumas, *père*, called *Kean*, a play on the life of the British actor Edmund Kean.

Having discarded that idea, Verdi invited Piave to work on an adaptation of Victor Hugo's play *Le Roi S'Amuse* (*The King Amuses Himself*), which he'd already shown a certain interest in with Salvatore Cammarano. Piave accepted and, ingenuously, assured Verdi that the Austrian censors certainly couldn't find anything to object to in a subject like this. Verdi and Piave got to work, but only three months before the premiere,

Rigoletto at the Teatro alla Scala, 1965–66 season. Directed by Margherita Wallmann, sets and costumes by Nicola Benois.

scheduled for February of 1851, the censors rejected the entire opera. Verdi, in Busseto, waited for Piave to resolve the situation in Venice.

Meanwhile Verdi defended his work, refusing to make any changes. This was an especially difficult period for Verdi! He found himself in the sights of two sniping enemies: on one side the Venetian censors, on the other the priggish citizens of Busseto, who found themselves deeply offended by the "scandalous" living arrangements of the unmarried Verdi and Strepponi.

In the end Verdi was forced to give in. Francis I, the libertine, immoral king in Hugo's play, was transformed into an anonymous duke of Mantua. It was also necessary to change the title of the work: *La Maledizione* (*The Curse*) was too immoral. The work therefore took the name of its protagonist, Rigoletto, even if in the original he's called Triboletto (Triboulet). Having overcome these and yet another series of endless intrusions by the censors, *Rigoletto* was finally ready and had its premiere on the evening of March 11, 1851, achieving an unconditional, absolute success. This opinion was repeated, immediately afterward, in the leading theaters in Italy, even if the opera was further censored, becoming from time to time *Viscardello*, *Clara di Perth*, or *Lionello*.

In *Rigoletto* the revolutionary choice of the character was immediately obvious: this is no longer an opera about an aristocrat, a lord, a warrior, or some other exalted personage. Instead there is a jester, complete with a hump. His is a complex, truly human psychology in which wickedness and the thirst for revenge are found side by side with a father's love. In this way the paradigm in which the tyrant is evil and the victim is good was smashed. The other leading players also show facets that make them at least ambiguous, while at the same time seeming almost banal on the basis of appearance. The handsome duke is in reality corrupt and immoral. Gilda herself is dangerously undecided between love and virtue, while the murderer Sparafucile has an unusual nobility.

Attention must also go, finally, to the increasingly obvious attention Verdi was paying to the "theatrical word," made clear by the theatrical "urgency," or better by the desire to flee musical conventions: he sought to unite arias, recitatives, duets, quartets, and other forms to make a drama that does not lose its unity, rhythm, and tension.

Above: Two figure drawings of the character Rigoletto. Edizioni Ricordi, Milan.

Left: Gilda, played by the soprano June Anderson, and Rigoletto, played by the baritone Leo Nucci, in Act II of the opera, Teatro La Fenice, Venice, 1992.

[...] In the theatrical version the story unfolds at the court of Francis I, where Triboulet nurtures, along with the corrupting profession of jester, a tender love for his daughter, Blanche, seduced by the king and killed by a murderer who was supposed instead to have avenged Triboulet. We know how Piave moved the story to Mantua and a different time. The major discovery of Victor Hugo (and this, we think, seduced Verdi) was the identification of the grotesque as a source of beauty. In the preface to *Cromwell* (1827) Hugo wrote, "What we call ugly, on the contrary, is a detail of a great whole which eludes us, and which is in harmony, not with man but with creation." And then: "An ugly thing, horrible, hateful, transported with honesty and poetry to the

Postcard with the final scene of Act III: Rigoletto discovers his dying daughter and remembers Monterone's curse.

kingdom of art, becomes beautiful, admirable, sublime, without losing one bit of its monstrosity."

It was precisely Triboulet's deformity that seemed to Verdi a mandatory artistic legitimization of his character. He wrote this to the president of La Fenice regarding proposed changes: "I observe finally that they have avoided making Triboletto ugly and hunchbacked. A hunchback who can sing? Why not!... Will it have an effect? I don't know; but if I don't know, I repeat,

neither does the person who proposed this modification. I thought it would be beautiful to portray this extremely deformed and ridiculous character who is inwardly passionate and full of love. I chose this subject for all these qualities, and if these original traits are removed, I will no longer be able to make music."

The prelude presents a perfect example of musical realism, of instrumental syllabification entrusted to horns. It is the monologue of Rigoletto remembering the curse ("Quel vecchio maledivami"— "That old man cursed me"), the decisive psychological passage of the opera, that has exclusive relevance at this moment, to the point that a single parenthesis (and a complete harmonic turn) in this instrumental prose opens at the twentieth beat.

The first scene of Act I is introduced by an offstage orchestra that evokes, with the flavor of a typical dance band, a sinister festivity. This is one of the most incisive and novel effects in Verdian literature, a musical connotation capable of suggesting a dramatic situation without defining it. This is truly a masterful invention for the allusion to an anxious atmosphere not specified by the music, expressed by brilliant means. With his infallible theatrical sensibility, after this stunning episode Verdi would again adopt this ambiguous musical stimulus, which by way of the greatest joy nonetheless suggests an impending but unknown catastrophe.

Within the climate of the opera, the newest invention in *Rigoletto* is the character of the duke of Mantua. Nothing about him is flattering in terms of sentiments and precedents from Verdi. But it is precisely this experiment, which goes beyond the categories of Verdian morality not crossed before, that establishes a new element in Verdi's imagination. There is something ambiguous and nearly dreadful in the duke's personality.

his fascination lies in the detachment he maintains unchanged amid the opera's events, just as his libertinism remains unscathed amid the tragedy, though it is very personal to Rigoletto and, in extremis, to Gilda.

In this sense his coherence is absolute, and we are far from affirming, as has been done, the existence of two planes in his personality: a dissolute and ambiguous one in the beginning and end of the opera, and a loving one, if not really passionate, said to emerge in Act II. Each of these distinctions seems groundless. The duke's central arias ("Ella mi fu rapita"—"She was taken from me," and "Parmi veder le lacrime"—"I seem to see tears"), while apparently more intense, serve to make more believable his impermeability to emotion, evident at the beginning and end with his distracted shamelessness. The duke's vocal structure confirms this reality with sufficient clarity. The only possible distinction is between his banal and intentionally boorish vocal character in the first and last acts and his finer vocal quality, traceable more to French examples than to Mozart, in Act II. The duke's character remains empty, but in the middle of the opera he sings beautiful music.

While there are undeniable musical novelties on the part of the duke, there is also no lack of them on Rigoletto's part. Rigoletto's case is not of someone oppressed or socially humiliated but of someone unhappy, frustrated. Hugo's Triboulet has the air of a Racinean tragedy, but Verdi moved the character to his own time, conceiving him against a background and a context that are bourgeois despite the noble setting. His is a private, very personal story that others are not prepared to understand: the story of a defeated man. His character was musically conceived by pushing the limits of traditional forms. He is presented with a

very new dramatic expression, recited, in which are inserted several emotional parentheses of intense sentimental abandon and great psychic tension, out of which emerges the cabalettism of "Sì vendetta." But this form is anything but mannerist. The transition from the lento "Piangi, fanciulla" ("Weep, my child") to the allegro vivo "Sì, vendetta" is not emphasized by a weak event that makes the succession obvious and immediate. Inserted between them is the episode of Monterone being led to prison, a highly important musical event that demonstrates how much freedom Verdi used in his composing.

Gilda is a character who remains behind the scenes, a slightly infantile character, who in Act III takes the initiative and on an impulse makes herself responsible for tragedy. Her vocal quality is that of a light soprano, more than a little affected, and only in the end, in the Act III quartet, is it possible to recognize her essential nature, which on the other hand is established by the other characters with an absolute precision in the musical characterizations that Verdi's genius maintained exactly in their proper dimensions.

Verdi never treats Sparafucile as an important character, despite the low F he sings, and as for Maddalena, she lives only in the musical context of others. The only aristocratic character in the opera is Monterone. One can find the inspiration from Mozart here and in other episodes. The citation is possible without forgetting the harmonic richness of Mozart and how the Verdian vocality makes little recourse to appoggiatura and passes instead along the notes of the chord, deriving from that the deep sense of worldliness. [...]

Duilio Couri
Guida all'Opera
Arnoldo Mondadori Editor

Il Trovatore

Dramma lirico in four parts to a libretto
by Salvatore Cammarano, completed by
Leone Emanuele Bardare, taken from the play
El Trovador by Antonio García Gutiérrez

FIRST PERFORMANCE
TEATRO APOLLO, ROME, JANUARY 19, 1853

FIRST PERFORMERS
ROSINA PENCO (LEONORA), EMILIA GOGGI (AZUCENA),
CARLO BAUCARDÉ (MANRICO), GIOVANNI GUICCIARDI (COUNT DI LUNA),
ARCANGELO BALDERI (FERRANDO)

CHARACTERS

Count di Luna, a nobleman of the kingdom of Biscay (*baritone*)

Leonora, lady-in-waiting to the princess of Aragon, betrothed to Count di Luna but in love with Manrico (*soprano*)

Azucena, a gypsy of Biscay, believed to be Manrico's mother (*mezzo-soprano*)

Manrico, officer of the prince of Biscay (*tenor*)

Ferrando, captain of the count's army (*bass*)

Ines, Leonora's confidante (*soprano*)

Ruiz, a soldier in Manrico's service (*tenor*)

An old gypsy (*bass*)

A messenger (*tenor*)

CHORUSES AND EXTRAS
Companions of Leonora, relatives of the count, men at arms, nuns, gypsies

TIME: Early 15th century.
PLACE: Spain, partly in Biscay, partly in Aragon.

Above: The mezzo-soprano Adelaide Borghi-Mamo in the costume of Azucena, a role for which she was famous.

Right: *Il Trovatore*, Teatro alla Scala, Milan, 1967. Conducted by Gianandrea Gavazzeni, directed by Luchino Visconti, sets and costumes by Nicola Benois.

PLOT

Background Events

Many years earlier, the elderly count di Luna had an old gypsy arrested when the wet nurse found her near the cradle of his second son. The boy, believed to be bewitched, languished from an all-consuming fever. Although the gypsy claimed innocence, the count condemned her to the stake, but her daughter managed to take the child. A few days later, a baby's charred remains were found where the gypsy had been burnt. All believed this was the count's stolen child.

Part I—The Duel

The old count has died and his surviving son has inherited the title. The young count has decided to marry Leonora, who, despite her promise, loves a mysterious soldier who presents himself to her as a troubadour. One night, while Leonora listens rapt to the troubadour's serenade, the count surprises them and recognizes the mysterious cavalier as Manrico, a follower of Urgel, pretender to the throne of Biscay, long condemned to death. The two face off in a duel; Manrico is seriously wounded and left for dead.

Part II—The Gypsy

A rocky locale in the mountains of Biscay. Azucena, daughter of the gypsy burnt at the stake by the elderly Count di Luna, has raised Manrico as her son.

Left: Scene from Part II of the 1967 La Scala production. At the center, the tenor Carlo Bergonzi in the title role. The other performers include the soprano Gwyneth Jones, the mezzo-soprano Fiorenza Cossotto, and the baritone Giangiacomo Guelfi.

Below: Playbill of *Il Trovatore* from New York City, 1867.

Now she heals the wounds he received in the duel. In the gypsy encampment, after listening to a dark and delirious song by Azucena, obsessed by the image of the stake and her mother, he asks her to tell him the story of those events. Azucena recreates the horrible scene, including a hand that pushed the baby into the fire only to then discover, with horror, that the baby killed was her own son, and the baby left alive the count's son.

The stupefied Manrico asks, "I'm not your son?" Azucena seeks to reassure Manrico, telling him that the memory of those events has put senseless words in her mouth. She encourages him to tell a story of his own, and Manrico narrates the story of his duel with the count. When he was about to strike his rival, a mysterious voice directed him not to hurt him.

In that moment a messenger arrives to tell Manrico that Leonora, believing him dead, is about to enter a convent. Deaf to his mother's exhortations, the young man sets off to dissuade Leonora.

In the cloister of a convent near Castellor. The Count di Luna also arrives to steal away the girl. The two rivals again find themselves face to face, but this time Manrico, with the help of a crowd of followers, has the upper hand and flees with Leonora.

Part III—The Gypsy's Son

Encampment of the Count di Luna. The army has besieged Castellor, where Urgel's rebels, led by Manrico, have taken refuge. Several soldiers surprise and capture a gypsy near the camp. She is brought to the count and Ferrando, who recognizes her as Azucena, the woman who stole the count's younger

A scene from *Il Trovatore* from the film *Senso* by Luchino Visconti, 1954.

brother. When he then discovers that Azucena is also the mother of Manrico, the count has the perfect opportunity to avenge the death of his brother and strike his rival: he commands his men to prepare a stake for burning.

At Castellor, before the decisive battle, Manrico wants to marry Leonora. Ruiz, a follower of Manrico, announces that Azucena has been captured. Manrico reveals to Leonora that the gypsy is his mother and then rushes off toward the enemy camp to save her.

Part IV—The Execution

A wing of the Aliaferia palace. The attempt to save Azucena has failed, and Manrico is imprisoned and condemned

to death. Leonora is prepared to do anything to save him. The Count di Luna gives orders to execute Manrico and his mother at dawn; undone, Leonora offers herself to the count in exchange for freedom for Manrico, but she secretly takes poison.

Interior of the prison. Azucena and Manrico await their deaths. Azucena is terrified by the idea of dying at the stake, but Manrico comforts her and she falls asleep.

Leonora arrives with the news of Manrico's freedom, but he intuits the price paid for his life, refuses the gift, and curses the woman. The poison soon begins to have its effect: Manrico understands the power of Leonora's love, while the Count di Luna realizes he has been tricked.

When Leonora has died, the count orders that Manrico be immediately executed and drags Azucena with him so she can witness the suffering of her son. Only when the youth has been decapitated does Azucena reveal that the count, in killing Manrico, has just killed his own brother.

BACKGROUND AND ANALYSIS

Since the spring of 1851 Verdi and Strepponi had been living on the estate of Sant'Agata, in a small house that underwent modifications and enlargements over the years. Far from gossip and immersed in the peace of the countryside, Verdi was finally able to dedicate himself only to subjects he liked, without worrying about whether they would be performed.

He had already put two librettists to work: Cammarano was busy with *El Trovador* by the Spanish author Antonio García Gutiérrez, and he had proposed to Piave what he called "a simple, affectionate subject" (the future *La Traviata*).

Verdi had long ago moved past the deference he had originally given Cammarano, and when he wasn't satisfied with the first draft of the libretto he immediately clarified his vision of the opera, following an epic-narrative outline. It is precisely from this viewpoint that *Il Trovatore* (*The Troubadour*) came into being and from which it should be interpreted, the entire opera immersed in a perennial and unreal nocturnal atmosphere. It is a silent night, as the characters themselves reaffirm several times: "Tacea la notte placida" ("The peaceful night was silent"), Leonora sings; "Tace la notte" ("The night is silent"), repeats the Count di Luna. Here there are no storms, as in *Rigoletto*; instead, as witness to the stories of the various characters, there is only the motionless night.

The opera begins with Captain Ferrando narrating the background events. It is then the turn of Leonora, who recounts her past meeting with the troubadour. In the aria "Condotta ell'era in ceppi" ("She was led in shackles"), Azucena, with her characteristic obsessiveness, unites the past to the present. This is followed by Manrico, who, in "Mal reggendo all'aspro assalto" ("Poorly bearing the harsh assault"), tells of his

Left: A famous oleograph by Luigi Morgari for *Il Trovatore.*

Below: The tenor Franco Corelli, one of the most acclaimed interpreters of Manrico, in a production of the opera at the Teatro alla Scala in 1963. Conducted by Gianandrea Gavazzeni, directed by Giorgio De Lullo, sets and costumes by Pier Luigi Pizzi.

Drawing by Romolo Liverani for *Il Trovatore*, 1853, in the Biblioteca Comunale, Faenza.

The soprano Gabriella Tucci in a production of *Il Trovatore* at New York's Metropolitan Opera; she was also the lead in a famous recording done in 1964 along with Franco Corelli, conducted by Thomas Schippers.

duel with the count. Only in Part III, when Azucena is captured, do past and present come together and unite, and from that moment on the story moves into its tragic and inevitable present.

In contrast to the night, dark and enveloping but also cold and nearly lifeless, there is another constant element: fire. Besides the stake, which obsesses Azucena, there is also the ardor in the characters' passions. "Perigliosa fiamma tu nutri" ("You feed a dangerous flame"), says Ines to Leonora, who, before dying, exclaims, "La mano è gelo" ("The hand is cold"), but then, touching her chest, "Fuoco orribile arde" ("A horrible fire burns here"). And again the Count exclaims, "Ah, l'amorosa fiamma m'arde ogni fibra" ("Ah, the flame of love burns my every fiber").

In *Il Trovatore* one breathes an atmosphere that we could define as that of an "epic-romantic ballad," and in that context the characters reclaim a language that Verdi seemed to have completely eliminated, a newly schematic dis-course composed of recitative, aria, and cabaletta. But this is only proper for this dark fable, so absolutely outside time.

With *Il Trovatore* Verdi's collaboration with Salvatore Cammarano came to a fatal end. In July of 1852 the librettist died, his work unfinished. Completion of the libretto, based on Cammarano's notes, fell to Leone Emanuele Bardare, a Neapolitan writer. Verdi finished the score in December of 1852, and the work premiered on January 19, 1853, at the Teatro Apollo in Rome. The success was enormous and the public rushed en masse to the theater, even though the Tiber, flooding at several points, threatened to put the premiere at risk. This opera's overwhelming power, so potent and immediate, won out over the power of water!

From *Trovatore* to *Trouvère*

In 1854, while Verdi was in Paris for performances of *Les Vêpres Siciliennes*, the Théâtre Italien staged *Il Trovatore*. The first-rate cast included Erminia Frezzolini (Leonora), Adelaide Borghi-Mamo (Azucena), and Francesco Graziani (Count di Luna). Verdi had the opportunity to attend the rehearsals, and regarding the performances (the first was on December 26, 1854), he wrote in a letter to De Sanctis, "I haven't written about *Il Trovatore* here; besides, you will know how things went. I know only that there were ten performances in a row (which never happens) and that the theater, especially on the last four nights, was very crowded."

After the success of *Les Vêpres Siciliennes* at the Opéra on June 13, 1855, the theater's management asked Verdi for a "grand-opéra"–style version of *Il Trovatore*. Thus began a long period of negotiations. Verdi was attentive not only to the financial aspects, but also to the quality of the production: he

wanted the theater to promise suitable performers and staging. It took until the autumn of 1856 for all obstacles to be overcome, and then rehearsals began for *Le Trouvère,* translated into French by Émilien Pacini.

All the performers were first-rate: Louis Guéymard (Manrique), Pauline Guéymard-Lauters (Léonore), Adelaide Borghi-Mamo (Azucena), and Marc Bonnehée (Comte de Luna). The opera opened on January 12, 1857, to a positive response from the public and critics. This French *Trovatore* shows careful refinement in the orchestration, which is more polished and precise. In Act III, after the soldiers' chorus, Verdi inserted a ballet, obligatory for the Paris stage. In Act IV Leonora's cabaletta "Tu vedrai che amore in terra" ("You will see that never on earth") is eliminated, as is often done even in the Italian version. The finale is completely new: after Leonora's death, events reach a conclusion very rapidly in the Italian version; in the French, as Manrique is led to the scaffold, there is a reprise of the "Miserere" chorus, over which is a short dialogue between Manrique and Azucena, while the orchestra evokes the theme sung by Léonore and Manrique during the "Miserere." There is a drum roll and the count drags the gypsy over to witness the troubadour's death.

Above: The first scene of Part II of *Il Trovatore* at the Teatro alla Scala, 1967. In the photo are the tenor Franco Corelli (Manrico) and the mezzo-soprano Fiorenza Cossotto (Azucena). The soprano Antonietta Stella and the baritone Ettore Bastianini also performed in this production.

Left, inset: The garden of the villa of Sant'Agata.

[. . .] In March of 1851, even before the premiere of *Rigoletto*, *Il Trovatore* first appeared in Verdi's correspondence when he proposed the subject to Salvatore Cammarano, librettist of *Alzira*, *La Battaglia di Legnano*, and *Luisa Miller*. Since the triumph of *Lucia di Lammermoor* (1835), Cammarano—actor, painter, and playwright—was seen in the world of melodrama as the only star worthy of being set beside Felice Romani. So Verdi, who routinely browbeat librettists like Solera and Piave, treated Cammarano with the proper deference, recognizing him as a noble man of letters and even respecting his ideas on theater without impatiently imposing his own. After *Luisa Miller* Cammarano was Verdi's librettist of choice. In December of 1849 Verdi had entrusted him with adapting *Re Lear*, and from him he expected "something worthy of him and of the subject we're handling; something with good sense, a rare commodity in the theater, but even so worthy of being attempted by artists with consciences like Cammarano and me," as he wrote their mutual friend Cesarino De Sanctis. Since he avoided the rushed life of the hack writer, the following March Cammarano declined to quickly adapt Victor Hugo's *Le Roi S'Amuse*, for which Verdi fell back on the faithful Piave.

But Cammarano was bound to Verdi by contract for a libretto, and Verdi now proposed to him *El Trovador* by Antonio García Gutiérrez, a chivalric romance enjoying popularity in Europe in which all the ingredients of Romantic excitement (duels, abductions, brigands, deaths) follow one another untidily, amalgamated by the lyrical passion of the language. A popular play par excellence, it had been first performed on a memorable evening in 1836, which ended with the author being summoned for a curtain call, a new event in the history of theatrical customs. *El Trovador* became an obligatory piece among the itinerant theatrical troupes that shaped popular taste in the 19th century, traveling from the cities to the villages in the provinces.

Twenty days went by, during which Cammarano gave no sign of life, made no response to Verdi's proposal; and when he was finally heard from it was indirectly, by way of De Sanctis, who told Verdi that the great man of letters had objections "as much for good sense as for the theater."

By way of the same intermediary Verdi responded, on March 29, 1851, and did so with aggressive force: "The more novelty Cammarano presents me, the freer the forms, the better I shall do. Let him do what he wants: the bolder he is, the happier he will make me. Let him only keep in mind the demands of the public, who want brevity. To you, then, who are his friend, urge him to not waste a moment of time."

In response to this advice Cammarano mailed back his synopsis, an outline of the libretto with its distribution into a suitable number of set pieces (cavatinas, romances, cabalettas, arias, duets, trios, concertati). On April 9, Verdi wrote Cammarano a letter in which—after calling him a "man of talent and superior character"—he reviewed the synopsis point by point. He suggested changes that removed the characters' last remnants of psychological development and made them stand out as bearers of passions sculpted by axe blows. So he preferred that Manrico not be injured in the duel with the Count di Luna ("This poor Troubadour has so little for himself that if we take away valor, what remains to him?") and that Azucena not lose her mind in the finale ("We must preserve to the end this woman's two great passions: her love for Manrico and her ferocious thirst to avenge her mother").

Nothing remained for Cammarano but to go to work, and for Verdi but to find a company willing to extend money and provide suitable performers. A new situation in his career, *Il Trovatore* was the first work he had set in motion without having reached agreements with a publisher and an impresario. He could therefore spend a year and a half in search of the ideal text, a series of verses that unequivocally contained the dramatic position of the events and the characters, whose inflections would directly evoke the musical intonation. The drafting of the score would then be a matter of how fast he could write it down. As Verdi told Quintino Sella during an idle moment in parliament, the question consisted of "writing down quickly enough the musical thoughts in the integrity with which they had come to mind." One might almost believe the impresario Benjamin Lumley, who in *Reminiscences of the Opera* claims that Verdi beat the famous speed of Rossini and sketched out *Il Trovatore* in ten days.

The exemplification of this way of working emerges from Verdi's correspondence with the librettist and the theaters. While thanking Cammarano for his poetic submissions ("Continue *Il Trovatore* as you have done the introduction and I'll call myself immensely happy"), since September of 1851 he'd been thinking of the demands of the vocal roles. He rejected La Fenice because he "needed first and foremost a tenor without objection" and weighed with Cammarano the possibility of Rome or Naples, depending on the opportunity to have "an actress for Azucena, for this Azucena I care about so much!"

This dragged on until June of 1852 before he reached a preliminary agreement with Jacovacci, impresario of the Apollo in Rome, provided that he was satisfied with Rosina Penco (the first Leonora), that they found another prima donna for Azucena, and that he was not pestered by the censors. The censors were a true irritation, and Jacovacci had been passing their demands on to Cammarano since November of 1851, convinced that "the leading melodramatic poet of the day" could make the audience understand that Leonora takes refuge in a cloister "without mentioning church, convent, or vows"; that the witch's condemnation was unrelated to the stakes of the Inquisition; that a civil war was going on, even if he was prohibited from naming exiles, parties, and factions; and so on. Cammarano had no difficulties making these changes, and so the story of *Il Trovatore* is thoroughly imprecise in terms of time and location.

As these negotiations concerning *Il Trovatore* neared their conclusion, Cammarano died before he could make the final changes to the libretto requested by the censors

and by Verdi. His student Leone Emanuele Bardare assumed his role. Verdi was getting better at making his requests precise. It was Bardare who redid the "characteristic song of Azucena (which I could play with, musically speaking, at several places in the drama)"—the famous image of "the roaring flames" in the beginning of "Stride la vampa" ("The blaze roared")—who wrote the baritone's "Il balen del suo sorriso" ("The flashing of her smile") and who approved the cuts and the versification made by Verdi based on Cammarano's sketches for the finales of the second and last parts.

Having signed the contract in November of 1852, Verdi declared he had finished the opera on December 14; on Christmas he was in Rome for the rehearsals. It premiered at the Apollo on January 19, 1853, with triumphant results. […]

Gioacchino Lanza Tomasi,
Guida all'Opera,
Arnoldo Mondadori Editore

Two 19th-century images of *Il Trovatore*: a lithograph for Part I (opposite) and a scene by Alfonso Goldini for a production at the Teatro Regio, Turin, in 1886.

La Traviata

Melodramma in three acts to a libretto by
Francesco Maria Piave, taken from the play
La Dame aux Camélias by Alexandre Dumas, *fils*

FIRST PERFORMANCE
TEATRO LA FENICE, VENICE, MARCH 6, 1853

FIRST PERFORMERS
FANNY SALVINI-DONATELLI (VIOLETTA), LODOVICO GRAZIANI (ALFREDO),
FELICE VARESI (GERMONT)

CHARACTERS

Violetta Valéry, a courtesan (*soprano*)
Flora Bervoix, her friend (*mezzo-soprano*)
Annina, Violetta's maid (*soprano*)
Alfredo Germont (*tenor*)
Giorgio Germont, his father (*baritone*)
Gastone, Vicomte de Letorières (*tenor*)
Baron Douphol, Violetta's protector (*baritone*)
Marquis d'Obigny, Flora's protector (*bass*)
Doctor Grenvil (*bass*)
Giuseppe, Violetta's servant (*tenor*)
A servant of Flora (*bass*)
A commissioner (*bass*)

CHORUSES AND EXTRAS
Ladies and gentlemen, friends of Violetta and Flora, matadors, picadors, gypsies, servants of Violetta and Flora, masked people

TIME: Around 1850.
PLACE: Paris and its environs.

PLOT

Act I

The sumptuous salon of Violetta Valéry in Paris. Violetta is offering her friends a brilliant party. Alfredo

toast and Violetta responds, welcoming the pleasure without a thought. While the guests leave the room, Violetta, suffering from consumption, is suddenly struck by a spell. Left alone,

Above: The soprano Cecilia Gasdia in the *La Traviata* by Franco Zeffirelli, Teatro Comunale, Florence, 1985.

Germont, who nurtures a secret and sincere love for her, is presented to her. When seated at table, the young man reveals his feelings with a passionate

she gazes with dismay at her pallor. Turning, she realizes Alfredo is still there, and he, after gently reproaching her for the frivolous life that is consuming her, asks for her love. At first Violetta is amused, but she then realizes that his words are sincere. Day is dawning, the guests take their leave, and with them also Alfredo departs. Left alone, Violetta reflects on his words.

Act II

A house in the country outside Paris. Violetta and Alfredo have been living together happily for about three months, far from the fashionable world of Paris. In order to continue their dream of love, Violetta has been selling her belongings, piece by piece. When he learns of this from Annina, Alfredo is beset by remorse and decides to atone for his thoughtlessness by going to the city in search of money. During his absence, Violetta is visited by Giorgio Germont: he forces her to leave Alfredo, who he believes has been drawn into ruin by a woman of easy morals. He is disturbed when he learns that it is not his son who is maintaining Violetta, but she who is selling her belongings to make possible their life together. The old Germont understands that Violetta is animated by sincere love and, making use of this nobility of spirit, he asks her to sacrifice herself to save the marriage of his daughter, whose betrothed refuses to marry as long as the scandalous relationship continues.

Violetta refuses at first, but in the end, in tears, she gives in. When Germont leaves, the unhappy Violetta writes a note to Alfredo and sets off for Paris. When Alfredo reads the note he is shocked. His father, who meanwhile has returned, seeks to console him, but Alfredo is gripped by jealousy and is more than anything determined to get revenge.

Opposite, top: Flora's home in Act II of *La Traviata*, Teatro La Fenice, Venice, 1990. Conducted by Roberto Abbado; direction, sets, and costumes by Pier Luigi Pizzi.

Above: Title page of the libretto in an edition published by Ricordi.

Below: Tiziana Fabbricini and Roberto Alagna in a 1990 La Scala production.

A party in Flora's town house. Violetta is a guest, accompanied by her onetime protector, Baron Douphol. Also arriving is Alfredo, who seems indifferent to the presence of Violetta and plays cards with the baron, but in reality is irritated by the presence of his rival. In an atmosphere heavy with tension, a servant announces that dinner is ready and everyone calms down, at least for the moment. Violetta turns to Alfredo and begs him to leave the party. He makes it conditional on her following him. Violetta, with a broken heart, remembering what she has promised Germont,

responds that she cannot and confesses that she is in love with Douphol. This unleashes the fury of Alfredo, who calls to his friends, and to prove that he has no ties to Violetta, he throws money at her. The brutal gesture arouses general indignation, and Germont has hard words for his son, while the baron challenges Alfredo to a duel.

Act III

Violetta, devoured by consumption, is near the end of her life. The doctor seeks to comfort her with compassion-

ate words, but she knows her life is at its end and despairs of being able to see Alfredo again, as Giorgio Germont has written to her: Alfredo has been told the truth by his father. Moved by Violetta's sacrifice and anguished at the injustice committed, he arrives at the bedside of his beloved. The happiness of the meeting gives Violetta a moment of serenity, but soon after—when she would like to get dressed, go out, and begin to live again—she suffers another collapse.

The end is near. Surrounded by Alfredo, Germont, Annina, and the doctor, Violetta dies in the arms of her beloved.

Opposite, top: Period illustration showing the character of Germont.

Above left: Drawing by Lila De Nobili for Act II of *La Traviata*, Teatro alla Scala, Milan, 1956.

Above: Title page of the play *La Dame aux Camélias* by Alexandre Dumas, *fils.*

Opposite, bottom: The soprano Giusy Devinu and the tenor Roberto Alagna in Act I of *La Traviata*, Teatro La Fenice, Venice, 1990.

Left: The Violetta/Germont duet in Act II. Conducted by Luchino Visconti, performed at Covent Garden, London.

BACKGROUND AND ANALYSIS

Verdi left Rome to return to Busseto after the third performance of *Il Trovatore*. A few months later, *La Traviata* (*The Fallen Woman*) was scheduled to open in Venice. Thus these two operas, diametrically opposed in subject and atmosphere, were divided by only a short period. Francesco Maria Piave worked on the libretto for this subject Verdi called "simple, affectionate," which was none other than an adaptation of the play *La Dame aux Camélias* (*The Lady of the*

Inset: Eighteenth-century costume for *La Traviata* in a period illustration.

Below: The soprano Giusy Devinu and the tenor Roberto Alagna in Act III of *La Traviata*, Teatro La Fenice, Venice, 1990.

aristocratic woman, daughter of a sovereign or similar. And the setting was contemporary. They had to find a way to dodge the censors' onslaught and avoid repeating the experience with *Rigoletto*.

With great adroitness, Verdi and Piave eliminated every verbal cue that could have revealed Violetta's actual profession, just as it was important to avoid overly explicit references to her illness. On the other hand, the "bourgeois" setting was emphasized, above all through the element of money, which runs through-

Camellias), by Alexandre Dumas, *fils*. Piave and Verdi worked rapidly on the libretto, taking suitable precautions. They certainly knew their subject was "touchy," their main character being a prostitute, albeit one at a high level, but even so a *mondana*, as was the Italian euphemism, and most certainly not an

out the opera. In Act II this aspect becomes highly evident in the dialogue between Alfredo and Annina; at the beginning of the duet of Germont and Violetta, with that "Pur tanto lusso" ("Such luxury"); up to what is the climax, "Qui pagata io l'ho" ("See that I have paid her") of Alfredo, the only

quantifying herself in money, all that remains are "dieci luigi," and now those ten golden coins are her value. This detail would suffice to rank Violetta among the most beautiful figures in the history of melodrama, given her complex psychology and moving humanity.

It was a story and a protagonist too "strong" and "modern" to be immediately understood. Thus, moved against Verdi's wishes to 18th-century Paris, and with inadequate performers, on March 6, 1853, the opera was a failure. After the disaster Verdi wrote to Muzio: "*La Traviata* last night: fiasco. Was the fault mine or the singers'? . . . Time will judge." And to Angelo Mariani: "*La Traviata* was a fiasco; what is worse, they laughed. Still, what can I say? I'm not upset. Am I wrong or are they? I myself believe that the last word on *La Traviata* was not heard last night. They will hear it again and we shall see. Meanwhile, dear Mariani, note the fiasco."

And time has amply judged the greatness of *La Traviata*, one of the best loved and most performed works in the lyric repertory of all time.

Above and opposite: Two moments from Act I of the La Fenice 1979 production of *La Traviata*. The photos show the soprano Jolanta Omilian (Violetta) and the tenor Beniamino Prior (Alfredo).

sharply realistic concession, in which Violetta's vocation also emerges. Only at the end, when our heroine, dying, orders Annina to bring some of the little money left to her, the phrase "Oh, mi sarà bastante" ("Oh, for me it will be enough") rings out, more emblematic than ever, veined with a sad irony. Of her life, lived

[...] In reading *La Traviata*, one sees that its tripartite form, regardless of the widespread performance practice, is imposed by the musical structure. Every reservation concerning this point must fall (as happens in German theaters, where Act I and the first scene of Act II are fused, dividing the opera with a single intermission) when faced with the profound tonal fracture detectable between Act I and Act II and at the *ad libitum* fermata that ends Act I. A quasi-invitation to perform the first and second scenes of Act II without a break comes from an imagined tonal relationship, well understood as an expressive relationship, recognizable between the two scenes, from the fact that the end of the first and the beginning of the second hit in at the same tempo and that the figure that closes the first is a measured fermata. The material is further clarified by the variations between the first prelude and the prelude to Act III (the first pitched major, the second minor), of decisive importance to the opera's expressive trajectory. The first prelude is on an idyllic theme, the second on a catastrophic one. All these emotions—as early as the opening prelude—are identified. The presentation of the phrase "Amami, Alfredo" ("Love me, Alfredo") is the central point, the wall of fire, the decisive psychological turning point in the opera. In fact, the theme of *La Traviata* cannot be identified as an attack on bourgeois society, although that theme exists in the opera, nor are its ideas drawn from a pamphlet on the customs of 19th-century Paris concocted from Dumas's novel. The social statement makes an indirect appearance, but the true meaning of *La Traviata* is in

Violetta's powerful ability to love, in the way she realizes herself in that emotion by way of passion and renouncement. That "Amami, Alfredo," expressed in the prelude, is therefore a sentimental passage to which all the rest of the opera is closely connected, musically and psychologically, an event from which the entire accumulation of later events will develop, each one inside the next.

By the prelude of Act III events are still taking place, but they have the substance of memory. The phrasing still bears an identification with Violetta's sentiments, still capable of a charge of affection and although pallid, of hope. But the culmination of the prelude, at the twenty-ninth beat, and also for two measures, belongs to the mind of Verdi: it is a phrase that with torment, speaks of the separation from life, of the destiny to be fulfilled.

Act I essentially presents a single situation, that being love, the expansion of an idyll. In Act II the dominion of action prevails. The entire act is taken up by a succession of events, happenings that would be difficult to place in any formal category. In Act III love is reborn but only for the leave-taking, to precipitate toward outcomes no longer avoidable.

The dominant expression in *La Traviata* is psychologism. During those years first with *Stiffelio*, later with *Rigoletto* and then markedly with *La Traviata*, Verdi discovered the psychological truth that led to the interior of a musical discourse by way of vocalism and, in this without precedent, by the use of the instruments, the totality of the orchestra. The final act with the preeminence of recitative vocal parts that are almost spoken, is historically a major example of psychologism expressed through story.

The innovations introduced with *La Traviata* are explicitly peremptory. With this opera Verdi burst free of the chains

Title page of *La Dame aux Camélias* by Alexandre Dumas, *fils*, Paris, 1884.

LA DAME
AUX CAMÉLIAS
PAR
ALEXANDRE DUMAS FILS
DE L'ACADÉMIE FRANÇAISE

PRÉFACE
DE JULES JANIN

NOUVELLE ÉDITION
Entièrement revue et corrigée

PARIS
CALMANN LÉVY, ÉDITEUR
ANCIENNE MAISON MICHEL LÉVY FRÈRES
3, RUE AUBER, 3

1884
Droits de reproduction et de traduction réservés

imposed by the stage and did away with characters drawn from myth, as well as those from legend and history, to dedicate himself to the pure present. Violetta begins as a virtuoso and ends, literally, as an actress. In Act I the invention of her character is tied to traditional standards: the aria ("Ah, fors'è lui"—"Ah, perhaps it is he") and the cabaletta ("Sempre libera"—"Always free") constitute the definition of her form. In Act II Violetta makes herself clear musically in relationships with others, spending herself generously. Her singing, in the duet with Germont, is dynamic, woven of risky intervals, of syncopations, of harmonic unscrupulousness as much as Germont's vocal character seems melodically flat. In Act III, the traditional form is repeated only to smash it. "Addio, del passato" ("Farewell to the dreams of the past") and "Prendi, quest'è l'immagine" ("Take this, it is the portrait") stand between aria and recitative. A new form of "speaking" dominates the scene.

Verdi worked out the figure of Alfredo with a certain amount of personal interest and most certainly not without sympathy. His is the sincere role of a man in love, with all the slightly mechanical reactions of that role. In those years Verdi had discovered the lyric tenor (the duke of Mantua, Alfredo) and the psychological comedy of the voices. Alfredo has a more lyrical quality than the leading male tenors found in later Verdi opera, such as Manrico or Radames. His personality is inferior to that of the duke, who has a coherent world of his own (although this is in truth a negative sign). Alfredo instead simply reacts to provocations in the obvious manner of a lover. Only in the last act do his extension and his vocal invention—with *agitato* in middle of a heartfelt phrase (as in "Parigi, o cara"—"Paris, O beloved"), a classic compositional procedure—confer on his character an overall sentimental relevance.

Giorgio Germont belongs to the "sketched-in" dimension of the theater, which Verdi opposed, the dimension that in terms of music can be called "Meyerbeerized." There is an avarice in his vocalism, a banality, as if he were the nervous depository of French musical philistinism. He represents the category of the conventional, the "others" in life, who always know the right word to use, remaining

completely aloof. Only in the last act, at the words "Ah, malcauto vegliardo!" ("Ah, rash old man!") with the insistence of the voice on the B-natural emphasized by the chromatic design of the orchestra, does his nature seem capable of sincerity.

As for the function of the chorus in *La Traviata*, there are certainly interesting usages, such as its perfect application in characterizing psychological situations (notable in this regard are the Matador Chorus and, most important, that of the Bacchanal), but it remains in the background and serves to awaken sensations in the characters or to animate the background. [...]

Duilio Courir,
Guida all'Opera,
Arnoldo Mondadori Editore

Sketch by Franco Zeffirelli for Act I of *La Traviata*, Teatro alla Scala, Milan, December 17, 1964.

Les Vêpres Siciliennes
(I Vespri Siciliani)

Dramma in five acts to a libretto by
Eugène Scribe and Charles Duveyrier

FIRST PERFORMANCE
THÉÂTRE DE L'OPÉRA, PARIS, JUNE 13, 1855

FIRST PERFORMERS
SOPHIE CRUVELLI (HÉLÈNE), LOUIS GUÉYMARD (HENRI),
MARC BONNEHÉE (MONTFORT), LOUIS-HENRI OBIN (PROCIDA)

CHARACTERS

Guy de Montfort (Montforte), governor of Sicily under Charles d'Anjou, king of Naples (*baritone*)
Le Sire de Béthune, French officer (*bass*)
Count de Vaudemont, French officer (*bass*)
Henri (Arrigo), a young Sicilian (*tenor*)
Jean (Giovanni da) Procida, a Sicilian doctor (*bass*)
Duchess Hélène (Elena), sister of Duke Frédéric of Austria (*soprano*)
Ninetta, her maid (*contralto*)
Daniéli, a Sicilian (*tenor*)
Thibault (Tebaldo), a French soldier (*tenor*)
Robert (Roberto), a French soldier (*bass*)
Mainfroid (Manfredo), a Sicilian (*tenor*)

Choruses and Extras
Sicilian men and women, French soldiers, penitents, executioner

Time: 1282.
Place: In and around Palermo.

Top right: A popular image of one of the first performers of *I Vespri Siciliani*.

Bottom right: Scene from Act II of *I Vespri Siciliani* at the Teatro Comunale of Bologna, 1986. Conducted by Riccardo Chailly, directed by Luca Ronconi, sets and costumes by Pasquale Grossi.

PLOT

Act I

The main square of Palermo. Several French soldiers sing and drink, watched over by Sicilians filled with hatred. The duchess Hélène makes her entrance, dressed in mourning for the death of her brother, killed by the French. Robert, one of the French soldiers, visibly drunk, insists that Hélène sing for them. Hélène intones a ballad that transforms itself into an incitement to rebellion. A riot ensues that is suppressed by the arrival of the French governor, Guy de Montfort.

Henri arrives, a young Sicilian of obscure origins. The governor decides to interrogate him, knowing he is emotionally tied to the duchess and suspecting he is plotting against the French. He asks him for information on his origins. Henri gives somewhat vague responses concerning his family, but reveals all of his hatred for the

French, and when Montfort orders him to stay far away from the duchess, in an act of defiance he sets off toward the duchess's palace.

Act II

A beach in the environs of Palermo. Jean Procida secretly returns to the city to organize a revolt against the French;

he is welcomed by Henri and Hélène. Together they assemble the alliances that will bring about the revolution, to which the king of Aragon will make a decisive contribution.

While Procida moves away, Henri declares his love for Hélène, but she tells him she will give hers only when the death of her brother has been avenged. Henri swears to it. A French officer brings Henri an invitation to the grand ball in the governor's palace. When the young man scornfully rejects the invitation, he is arrested. In a short time the scene becomes more animated. An engagement party is about to begin: young couples perform a vivacious tarantella, while several French soldiers begin harassing the women. Tempers begin to flare, and as a boat goes by carrying French officials and elegant women to the governor's ball, the Sicilians on the beach sing of their thirst for revenge.

Act III

In Montfort's study. The governor is reading a letter from a woman he seduced and abandoned years ago. Brought to Montfort, Henri is welcomed with great benevolence and expresses

his amazement at this welcome; soon, however, his wonder turns to emotional upheaval when he learns that he is standing together with his father; he is the child of the seduced woman. Devastated by this revelation that could make him lose Hélène's love, Henri rejects his father and rushes from the room.

In a hall of the same palace, the ball is about to begin. It is to open with a dance that represents "the four seasons." The guests dance, among them the masked Hélène, Procida, and other conspirators. Henri joins them and Hélène informs him that Montfort is about to be killed. The distressed young man can't decide whether he should alert his father and manages only to block the dagger blow that Hélène herself is about to deliver. Montfort has the conspirators arrested, and they rail against the traitor Henri.

I Vespri Siciliani, by Francesco Hayez, 1821–22, Galleria Nazionale d'Arte Moderna, Rome.

Above: The Paris Opéra, where *Les Vêpres Siciliennes* was premiered to notable public and critical success on the evening of June 13, 1855.

Below: Sketches by Pier Luigi Pizzi for the inauguration of the 1989–90 La Scala production of *I Vespri*.

Act IV

Henri meets Hélène in the fortress where the conspirators are imprisoned. First she rejects him, holding against him the presumed treason, but when she learns what drove him to act as he did her hatred transforms to pity. Henri and Hélène renew their promises of love and decide to die together. Procida enters along with all the condemned: the governor orders that they will be immediately executed, but Henri implores him to spare them. Montfort declares himself willing to pardon them, provided Henri recognizes him as his father and calls him by this name in front of everyone. After much hesitation, Henri gives in. Montfort gives his pardon and, to seal the newfound peace, announces the marriage of Henri to Hélène. There is general joy, in the midst of which, however, Procida is ready for a new action against the French.

Act V

In the gardens of the governor's palace, the celebrations are about to begin for the wedding of Henri and Hélène, which according to Montfort will lead to a period of peace and serenity. The completion of the rite will be saluted by the ringing of all the bells in the city. But it will not be a moment of joy. Procida announces to Hélène that it will signal the beginning of the massacre of the French. So it is that she finds herself in a dramatic position: betray the cause or lose herself and the man she loves.

Hélène, in sorrow, tries to avoid the ceremony. The distressed Henri curses her. But Montfort, without listening to Hélène's objections, insists that the marriage ceremony begin and orders that the bells ring. At the signal, the garden is invaded by armed Sicilians, who throw themselves at Montfort and the French.

BACKGROUND AND ANALYSIS

After the three works that became known as his "popular" or "romantic" trilogy—*Rigoletto*, *Trovatore*, and *Traviata*—Verdi seemed eager for a new direction. After eighteen operas in eleven frenetic years, he seemed finally to have reached a moment when he could slow the pace. But this did not mean he would stop, because he was driven by a creative energy that gave him no peace.

Together with his "Peppina"—of whom he said, very respectfully, "In my house lives a free woman, independent, a lover like me of the solitary life"—Verdi spent the spring and summer of 1853 at Sant'Agata, dedicating himself to his land, and once again the *Re Lear* project reemerged. The material he had prepared with Cammarano went to a new librettist, Antonio Somma, from Udine. Verdi had no lack of commitments. Already underway was a job for the

Above: Conductor James Levine, aside from conducting *I Vespri Siciliani* at the Metropolitan Opera in New York, recorded the opera in 1973 with the soprano Martina Arroyo, the tenor Plácido Domingo, the baritone Sherrill Milnes, and the bass Ruggero Raimondi. This was the first complete recording of Verdi's score.

Left: The final scene of the opera at La Scala, in the 1989–90 production. Conducted by Riccardo Muti; direction, sets, and costumes by Pier Luigi Pizzi.

Above: Riccardo Muti conducted *I Vespri Siciliani* at the Maggio Musicale Fiorentino in 1978 and at the Teatro alla Scala in 1989.

Below: Sketch by Pier Luigi Pizzi for the 1989–90 La Scala production of *I Vespri Siciliani*.

Opéra in Paris for the 1855 Exposition Universelle. After *Jérusalem*, which was a reworking of *I Lombardi*, Verdi had to write an opera especially for the Parisian stage, or as Verdi called the Opéra, the *grande bottega* ("great workshop"). In October of 1853, a few days after Verdi's fortieth birthday, he and Strepponi left for Paris.

Problems began right away. The Opéra's official librettist, Eugène Scribe, was running late on the deadline established (the detailed contract had called for the libretto to be ready in June of 1852), and he palmed off on Verdi a hardly appreciated "secondhand" libretto that was a reworking of the *Duca d'Alba* by Donizetti.

Verdi had before him a year to compose the music, an expanse of time that, given the working rhythms he'd followed before, could have been termed "enormous." But to him, that mattered little. To take on a rigidly codified genre like that of "grand opéra," with its formal requirements, including five acts, huge crowd scenes, and an obligatory ballet, was arduous work for a composer like him, naturally dedicated to dramatic synthesis; thus the composition went ahead with some difficulty. Even so, in October of 1854 a good part of the opera was finished and rehearsals began. After only a few days, however, the lead soprano, Sophie Cruvelli, the true star of the Opéra, disappeared.

The theater was in chaos, and Verdi, at war with Scribe, who was deaf to his requests for changes to the libretto, was exasperated. Then, as suddenly as she'd

disappeared, Cruvelli reappeared; meanwhile, however, the directors of the Opéra had been dismissed and replaced. Hector Berlioz wrote, "Verdi is also at odds with all the Opéra people. Yesterday there was a terrible scene with him at the dress rehearsal. I feel for the poor fellow, for I put myself in his place. Verdi is a noble and honorable artist."

previous productions." It was a judgment many agreed with. Verdi had managed to adjust to French conventions admirably, but the "true" Verdi showed up in how he took on the arias. A good example is the entrance of Hélène in Act I, in which recitative, aria, and cabaletta compose a formal block of great dramatic and theatrical power; but there are also the solo

Despite these vicissitudes, *Les Vêpres Siciliennes* (*The Sicilian Vespers*) had its premiere on the evening of June 13. Its success, both public and critical, was notable and rose to become triumphant with further performances. Berlioz wrote, "We must admit that in *Les Vêpres* the penetrating intensity of the melodic expression, the sumptuous variety, and the learned sobriety of the instrumentation, the fullness and the poetic sonorousness of the ensemble pieces, and the passionate but slow-developing force that forms one of the characteristic traits of Verdi's genius, give the entire work a certain stamp of grandeur, a sort of sovereign majesty more strongly marked than in any of the author's

moments for Montfort and Henri, which show strong introspective adherence expressed by a sharp handling of drama that is in no way overdone.

After the happy Parisian debut, Ricordi immediately thought of bringing *Les Vêpres Siciliennes* to Italy, and with Verdi's approval he entrusted the poet Arnaldo Fusinato with the Italian version of the libretto. As always, however, the zealous censors intervened, and once again an opera underwent continuous changes to its title and setting. To see *I Vespri Siciliani* in Italy with the original title and setting, one would have had to wait until 1861, at the Teatro Carolino in Palermo, by which time the Bourbons had been cast out.

Scene from Act I of *I Vespri Siciliani* at the Metropolitan Opera in New York, 1974. Conducted by James Levine. Principal performers: the soprano Montserrat Caballé (at the center of the photo), the tenor Nicolai Gedda, the baritone Sherrill Milnes, and the bass Justino Díaz.

Simon Boccanegra

Melodramma in a prologue and three acts
to a libretto by Francesco Maria Piave, later
revised by Arrigo Boito, taken from the play
Simón Bocanegra by Antonio García Gutiérrez

FIRST PERFORMANCE
TEATRO LA FENICE, VENICE, MARCH 12, 1857

FIRST PERFORMERS
LUIGIA BENDAZZI (MARIA), CARLO NEGRINI (GABRIELE),
LEONE GIRALDONI (BOCCANEGRA), GIACOMO VERCELLINI (PAOLO),
GIUSEPPE ECHEVERRIA (FIESCO)

CHARACTERS IN THE
PROLOGUE

Simon Boccanegra, corsair
in the service of the
Genoese republic (*baritone*)
Jacopo Fiesco, a Genoese
nobleman (*bass*)
Paolo Albiani, a Genoese
goldsmith (*baritone*)
Pietro, a Genoese popular
leader (*baritone*)

CHARACTERS IN THE
DRAMA
Simon Boccanegra, doge
of Genoa (*baritone*)
Maria Boccanegra, his
daughter, under the name
Amelia Grimaldi (*soprano*)
Jacopo Fiesco, under the
name of Andrea (*bass*)
Gabriele Adorno, a Genoese
gentleman (*tenor*)
Paolo Albiani, the doge's
favorite courtier (*baritone*)
Pietro, another courtier
(*baritone*)
A captain of crossbowmen
(*tenor*)
Amelia's maid (*soprano*)

CHORUSES AND EXTRAS
Soldiers, sailors, populace,
servants of Fiesco, senators,
the court of the doge

TIME: 1339 and 1363.
PLACE: Genoa and its
environs.

PLOT

Prologue

A square in Genoa on a night in September 1339. Simon Boccanegra, with support from Paolo Albiani, leader of the Plebeian party, is among the favorites for the position of doge. When Paolo proposes he try for election, Boccanegra is reluctant, but in the end he accepts: as doge he will be able to marry Maria, daughter of Jacopo Fiesco, thus legitimizing the baby girl born to them and entrusted to a wet nurse near Pisa. Fiesco strongly disapproves of the love affair and has imprisoned Maria in his palace for three months, and she has fallen seriously ill. Now Fiesco himself appears and announces that Maria is dead, cursing her seducer. Boccanegra, meanwhile, wanders near the palace

hoping to embrace Maria again and runs into Fiesco; he implores his pardon, but Fiesco is implacable and

declares himself ready to pardon Boccanegra only if he will give him the baby girl. Boccanegra says he returned from a trip to find the house abandoned, the wet nurse dead, and no sign of the baby. Full of hatred, Fiesco goes away. Boccanegra enters the palace and cries out in anguish at finding Maria's dead body.

Act I

The Grimaldi palace, near Genoa, in a garden with a view of the sea. Twenty-

five years have passed. It is dawn, and Amelia Grimaldi awaits her beloved, Gabriele Adorno. When he arrives, Amelia begs him to desist from the plot against the doge in which he is involved with Andrea Grimaldi, but they are interrupted by Pietro, who announces the arrival of the doge. Amelia believes the doge plans to force her to marry Paolo Albiani. She thus urges Adorno to speak with Andrea so he will hasten their wedding. When she leaves, Gabriele runs into Andrea, who in reality is Fiesco in disguise. Here we learn that Amelia Grimaldi is an orphan that he adopted to replace the real one—who died in a convent in Pisa—to keep the doge from confiscating the belongings of his family, fallen into disgrace for having conspired against Boccanegra. Gabriele, indifferent to this revelation, reaffirms his love.

Amelia and the doge meet. After performing an act of clemency with regard to the Grimaldi family, the doge

Opposite, top: Libretto of *Simon Boccanegra*.

Above: The riot in the second scene of Act I, as presented in a drawing by stage designer Carlo Ferrario.

Opposite, bottom: Bass Roberto Scandiuzzi in a scene from the prologue of *Simon Boccanegra* in the 1991 production at the Teatro La Fenice, Venice. Conducted by Roberto Paternostro; direction, sets, and costumes by Pier' Alli.

expresses his desire that Amelia marry Albiani. But the girl, encouraged by the doge's display of benevolence, confides to him that she is in love with another man and reveals that she is not the daughter of Andrea Grimaldi but an orphan from the area of Pisa. The doge realizes that the girl standing in front of him is the daughter he believed dead. When Amelia is gone, Boccanegra tells Paolo that he will have to give up Amelia's hand; furious, Paolo swears that he will get revenge; with the complicity of Lorenzino, he will abduct Amelia. The senate is in the council hall in the palace. While the doge invokes peace and brotherhood among Italian cities, the sounds of an uproar are heard from the square: Gabriele Adorno is being chased by the crowd. Boccanegra announces that he is ready to hear the reasons of the people. The common people break in with Gabriele and Andrea (Fiesco). The young man announces that he has killed Lorenzino for his attempt to abduct Amelia Grimaldi on the orders of an important politician. Gabriele

throws himself at the doge, who he believes is the one who organized the abduction: Amelia arrives and puts herself between the two. She asks pardon for Gabriele and relates how she was abducted and says she is ready to reveal the name of the planner of the abduction. A new tumult breaks out between the nobles and the plebeians. With difficulty the doge manages to get everyone calm and orders that Gabriele Adorno and Andrea are to be held in the palace; then, turning to Paolo and pretending to not know who was responsible for the attempted abduction, he forces him to join the unanimous cry of hatred against the guilty.

Act II

The doge's room in the ducal palace at Genoa. Seeking revenge, Paolo pours poison in the doge's water pitcher. After having Gabriele and Fiesco brought before him, he tries to prompt Fiesco to murder Boccanegra, insinuating to Adorno the suspicion that Amelia is the doge's lover. Amelia arrives and Gabriele accuses her, but the girl, unable to reveal the secret,

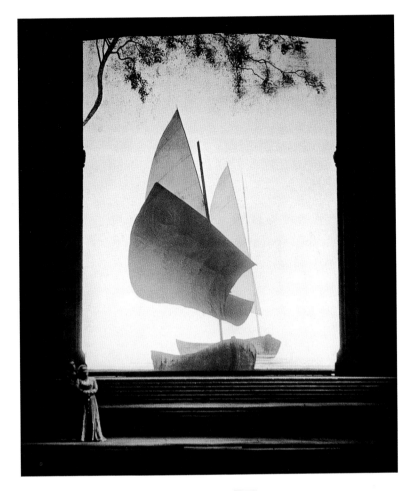

affirms that she has a "holy love" for the doge. Boccanegra enters and Gabriele hides. The girl confesses to her father that she loves Gabriele. The doge responds that the man she loves is a conspirator. Amelia begs him to pardon Gabriele, and then leaves.

Left alone, Boccanegra drinks a cup of water, sits down, and falls asleep. Adorno enters to stab him but is stopped by Amelia. Boccanegra suddenly awakens and reveals to Gabriele the true identity of Amelia. Gabriele asks pardon. From outside come sounds of an uprising. Adorno will not join the uprising, but will seek to avoid the useless spilling of blood. Boccanegra, as a reward for his loyalty, gives him the hand of Amelia.

Act III

A hall in the ducal palace. The revolt has finally been put down. Paolo is condemned to death, and while being brought to the scaffold to be executed he meets Fiesco, to whom he reveals that he poisoned Boccanegra.

While the sound of a wedding song grows stronger, the doge enters. The poison is having its effect, and his steps are unsteady. Fiesco sees this, reveals who he is, and announces that his enemy is about to die.

Boccanegra, with the detachment of someone who knows he no longer has anything to lose, asks to be forgiven, and to a visibly moved Fiesco reveals that Amelia is in reality Maria's daughter. At that point Amelia and

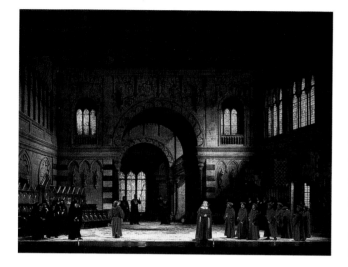

A scene from *Simon Boccanegra* at the Teatro Comunale of Florence in 1988. The stage sets were based on original sketches from 1881.

Gabriele arrive. The doge, nearing death, invites the girl to embrace Fiesco, her grandfather, and then he addresses the senators and dignitaries of the republic and orders that Gabriele Adorno be nominated his successor.

Rehearsals of *Simon Boccanegra* in a caricature by Melchiorre Delfico, today kept, along with many others, at the villa of Sant'Agata.

BACKGROUND AND ANALYSIS

In December of 1855 Verdi and Strepponi returned to Sant'Agata. Verdi had several projects and immediately got busy with *Stiffelio*, which he had to rework to eliminate problems with the censors for good. Verdi summoned Piave and entrusted him with the "dressing up" of the opera, which, as already noted, premiered at the Teatro Nuovo in Rimini in August of 1857. Meanwhile, negotiations were going on with the Teatro della Pergola in Florence and the San Carlo in Naples; Verdi dreamed of seeing the longed-for *Re Lear* performed at the latter. In March of 1856 Verdi went to Venice to follow a revival of *La Traviata* at La Fenice. While there he signed the commitment for his fifth Venetian opera, for the 1856–57 season. As was by then his habit, Verdi verified that the performers would be of the proper caliber and, further, asked for "some good *comprimarie* [singers in minor roles]."

The subject chosen was taken from another play by the Spaniard Antonio García Gutiérrez, entitled *Simón Bocanegra*, inspired by the doge of that name who ruled Genoa from 1339 to 1363, the year he was poisoned by a Genoese nobleman during a banquet. Verdi worked on *Boccanegra* while he was again in Paris, this time for the production at the Opéra of the French version of *Il Trovatore*. This proved a difficult undertaking, given the complexity of stagings for the Parisian theater, although this did not distract him from his work for La Fenice, as indicated by his extensive correspondence with Piave.

Unsatisfied with parts of Piave's text and pressed by the looming deadline, Verdi turned to Giuseppe Montanelli, a Tuscan politician and playwright in exile in Paris, for help reworking several scenes.

Even so, the work did not go quickly, and when Verdi returned to Italy, on January 12, 1857, it was still far from done. On February 18, when rehearsals began in Venice, one act was still lacking, along with the instrumentation.

Simon Boccanegra finally premiered on March 12 and was not a success with the public, while critics praised the dramatic coherence of the music, the elegant instrumentation, and an inspired use of melody, though there was some perplexity concerning overly "declaimed" singing and the complexity of the plot, which was not always clear.

The problem is that *Boccanegra* never got off the ground. There were equally negative outcomes at the Municipale in Reggio Emilia, the Pergola in Florence, the San Carlo in Naples, La Scala in Milan, the Carlo Felice in Genoa, and the Teatro Comunale in Bologna, all seeming to decree the definitive condemnation of *Boccanegra*, with no hope of appeal.

It is easy to understand this failure with the public. *Boccanegra* is an opera in which there is no abundance of arias, the title character doesn't have a single one, and those that exist have primarily dramatic value and would not excite the public. Twenty-three years later, the tireless Giulio Ricordi, after various fruitless attempts, managed to convince Verdi to rework the score.

Crucial to this was Verdi's meeting with composer/writer Arrigo Boito, resulting in an important collaboration that would produce Verdi's final masterpieces, *Otello* and *Falstaff*. Verdi and Boito began intense work on revising the opera, of which Verdi said, "I admit the table is shaky, but if we adjust the legs a bit, it will stand"; but he also said it was "like dealing with a new opera." Through the patient work of making connections and changes, Verdi managed to blend his styles of 1857 and 1881, intervening even more in the melodic curves of the singing to favor more intense dramatization. Some wholly new parts were added, including the grand scene of the council that ends Act I, where the chorus's role is anything but secondary. The entire opera is enclosed in an atmosphere of dark anxiousness, from which Boccanegra and Fiesco emerge and stand out. Finally, Verdi and Boito gave further prominence to the figure of Paolo, a true villain.

The two worked intensely through the winter of 1880 to 1881, and in the end *Simon Boccanegra* was ready to begin its new life. On the evening of March 24, 1881, the opera got its suitable consecration at La Scala, and Verdi could finally affirm "how well the legs had been adjusted on the old Boccanegra."

An intense Piero Cappuccilli, one of the greatest interpreters of the role of Boccanegra, in the 1971 La Scala production.

Un Ballo in Maschera

Melodramma in three acts to a libretto by
Antonio Somma, based on the play *Gustave III,
ou Le Bal Masqué* by Eugène Scribe

FIRST PERFORMANCE
TEATRO APOLLO, ROME, FEBRUARY 17, 1859

FIRST PERFORMERS
EUGENIA JULIENNE-DEJEAN (AMELIA), PAMELA SCOTTI (OSCAR),
ZELINA SBRISCIA (ULRICA), GAETANO FRASCHINI (RICCARDO),
LEONE GIRALDONI (RENATO)

CHARACTERS

Riccardo, count of Warwick, governor of Boston (*tenor*)
Renato, a Creole, Riccardo's secretary (*baritone*)
Amelia, Renato's wife (*soprano*)
Ulrica, a fortune-teller (*contralto*)
Oscar, a page (*soprano*)
Silvano, a sailor (*bass*)
Samuel, an enemy of the count (*bass*)
Tom, an enemy of the count (*bass*)
A judge (*tenor*)
Amelia's servant (*tenor*)

CHORUSES AND EXTRAS
Gentlemen, deputies, officials, guards, associates of Samuel and Tom, sailors, male and female citizens, servants, masked people, dancing couples

TIME: Late 17th century.
PLACE: Boston and its environs.

PLOT

Act I

A hall of the governor's house. Riccardo begins his audiences, but his mind is elsewhere: he is thinking of the woman with whom he is hopelessly in love, Amelia, wife of Renato, his secretary. Renato, meanwhile, reveals to him that plots are being hatched against him, but Riccardo refuses to listen to the names of the conspirators and acts magnanimously toward a black fortune-teller, Ulrica, accused of supernatural practices. Rather than ordering her exile, he decides to disguise himself and pay her a call.

Ulrica's poor dwelling. She is surrounded by people waiting to consult with her. Riccardo now arrives, disguised as a fisherman, and with great wonder sees one of Amelia's servants, who announces her mistress's visit. When everyone else has left, Ulrica receives Amelia, who begs her to find a cure for the amorous passion that torments her. Ulrica recommends an herb of forgetfulness that must be gathered at midnight near a gallows.

When Amelia leaves, Ulrica has everyone return and the disguised Riccardo consults the fortune-teller, asking about his future. Ulrica reveals that he is soon to die at the hand of a friend. With feigned nonchalance Riccardo seeks to dispel this prophecy and asks for the name of the murderer. The man who will first shake your hand, says Ulrica. Meanwhile Renato arrives and greets the governor by warmly shaking his hand.

The ball scene in Act III of the opera in a production at the Teatro Regio in Parma, 1998. Conducted by Angelo Campori, direction by Grazia Amarilli, sets and costumes by Pierluigi Samaritani.

Everyone believes the oracle lied. Having revealed his true identity and revoked the banishment of the fortune-teller, Riccardo is acclaimed by the people.

Act II

An empty field near Boston. While Amelia searches for the magical herb, Riccardo appears. Amelia begs him to leave her alone, but in the end she cannot hide her passion. Interrupted by Renato, who has come to save Riccardo from a group of conspirators coming there, Amelia manages to cover her face with a veil. Renato tells his friend the only escape route from the assassins, and Riccardo is convinced only after entrusting to Renato the veiled woman, with the promise that Renato will do nothing to

discover her identity. After Riccardo has gone, Samuel, Tom, and the other conspirators arrive. Surprised at not finding Riccardo, they want to reveal the identity of the mysterious woman, but Renato draws his sword, and Amelia, terrified,

Scene from *Un Ballo in Maschera* at the Teatro San Carlo, Naples, in 1859.

Left: Title page of the libretto of *Un Ballo in Maschera*, Milan, 1861.

Below: Postcard depicting the meeting of Ulrica and Riccardo in Act I.

intervenes, and her veil falls. While the conspirators snigger at this unique amorous encounter, Renato, wounded by the betrayal of his wife and friend, decides to join the conspirators and has them meet him the next day in his home. Then, as promised, he escorts Amelia into the city.

Act III

A room in Renato's house. He violently accuses Amelia, who must expiate her betrayal with death. She tries to prove her innocence and asks the favor of seeing their only son. Meanwhile, the conspirators arrive and with Renato they make a plan to kill Riccardo. Only one will be the avenger, chosen by lot. Amelia, who has returned to announce Oscar's arrival, unknowingly draws her husband's name, and from Renato's sinister delight she intuits that Riccardo's death is meant. Oscar brings the count's invitation to a masked ball, which the conspirators see as the occasion to carry out their plan.

Riccardo has sadly decided never to see Amelia again and has signed a decree allowing Renato to return to England with his family. Oscar enters with a card from a mysterious woman: it is a heartfelt appeal to the count not to attend the ball, for his life is in danger. But Riccardo has already decided: he will be there to see Amelia for the last time.

A sumptuous ballroom. Between music and dances, in the presence of the many guests, the ball is in full swing. Renato manages to learn from Oscar what costume Riccardo will be wearing. Riccardo, meanwhile, has met a masked woman: it is Amelia, who in tears exhorts him to immediately leave the ball. It is too late; Renato arrives behind them and stabs the count, but before dying Riccardo finds the strength to exonerate Amelia and to forgive everyone.

BACKGROUND AND ANALYSIS

In March of 1857, a few months after the premiere of *Simon Boccanegra*, Verdi completed the reworking of *Stiffelio*, which became *Aroldo*, performed at Rimini in August of the same year. The conductor was a young man for whom there were high hopes, a Ravenna native named Angelo Mariani; an outstanding musical personality, he was the first orchestra conductor in the modern sense, and Verdi was especially taken with this young artist's talents.

At performances of *Simon Boccanegra* and *Aroldo*, Verdi and Strepponi, for the first time, went against public opinion and appeared together. After all the years of keeping out of sight, the couple went out in the open, and on the occasion of the upcoming engagement in Naples, Verdi happily announced to a Neapolitan friend: "I'm coming to Naples with my wife!"

Verdi had a commitment with the Teatro San Carlo and had in mind *Re Lear*. He had reworked the libretto with the collaboration of Antonio Somma, but complications came his way from

The tenor Luciano Pavarotti, one of the most well-rounded and esteemed interpreters of the role of Riccardo.

the theater, which was unable to promise Verdi the cast he wanted, and the project was once again set aside.

So it was that Verdi had another project in mind when he left for Naples: a preexisting libretto by Eugène Scribe, *Gustave III, ou Le Bal Masqué*, set to music in 1833 by Daniel Auber, and translated and readapted by Salvatore Cammarano with new music by Saverio Mercadante in 1843, under the title *Il Reggente*. Three months before the date established for the premiere, Antonio Somma set to work on the new adaptation, entitled *Una Vendetta in Domino*. The creation of the text went ahead smoothly, and soon a copy was on the table of the Chamber of Revisions, the censors of the Neapolitan state. Thus began the umpteenth battle between censors and Verdi: on one side requests

for modifications, on the other explanations atop further explanations, all the while time going by. The premiere date came and went, the opera season ended, and Verdi found himself holding a libretto so thoroughly distorted even in its title, *Adelia degli Adimari*.

Sketches of costumes by Enrico Job for the La Scala production of *Un Ballo in Maschera* that opened the 1972–73 season.

The final scene of the opera in the 1998 production at the Teatro Regio in Parma. At the center are the tenor Salvatore Licitra (Riccardo) and the soprano So-Eun Serenelli (Oscar).

Right: Scene from *Un Ballo in Maschera*, Act I, first scene, Teatro Regio, Parma, 1998.

Below: Stage setting for scene three of Act III of *Un Ballo in Maschera*, by Oskar Kokoschka, 1963.

Verdi refused to compose music for this and decided to depart Naples for Rome, where a play in prose on the same subject was being performed without the slightest intervention from censors. The text thus got by the Roman censors, who gave their approval provided the story was moved to a country outside Europe, without sovereigns.

Verdi's patience was at its limit. He and Somma searched for a suitable location, even considering the Caucasus, and at last the choice fell on Boston in the 1600s, with the protagonist fashioned into a mere governor. Following new efforts to rework the text, and under the definitive title of *Un Ballo in Maschera* (*A Masked Ball*), the opera premiered at the Teatro Apollo on February 17, 1859, and met with great success. It was then that the cry "Viva Verdi!" spread, the letters of his name—V.E.R.D.I.—meant to indicate *Vittorio Emanuele Re d'Italia*: Victor Emmanuel, King of Italy. With *Un Ballo in Maschera* even the critics of the time noted that Verdi's work had taken

another important step forward: scenes blended into one another in rapid succession, and the "theatrical word" brought about a transformation of the aria into a kind of monologue, a sort of mirror of the soul. All by way of saying that the distinction between the so-called recitative and aria was imperceptible. The singing, syllabic and smoothed out, completely abandoned the habits of bel canto. What remained were the flourishes of the page Oscar: his brilliance made a purposeful contrast to the dramatic moments of the opera, as did the conspirators' jeers at the close of Act II, a sharp comment on the drama of Amelia and Renato. A contrast we also encounter in Riccardo's character—brilliant, ironic, but also melancholic and introspective.

After the effort to stage *Un Ballo in Maschera*, which had been far from easy, Verdi fell into a period of depression and discomfort. His letters make very clear his desire to abandon the stage and retire to the country.

The soprano Antonella Banaudi (Amelia) in Act II of the opera, Teatro Regio, Parma, 1998.

The baritone Alberto Gazale (Renato) and the basses Davide Peltretti (Samuel) and Marco Spotti (Tom), in the first scene of Act III of the opera, Teatro Regio, Parma, 1998.

[. . .] What seems to have interested Verdi initially was the court setting, the rococo splendor. This is why the intrusion of the censors, unable to countenance the depiction of a regicide, irritated him so much. It was proposed to him that he do an *Adelia degli Adimari* in place of the planned *Una Vendetta in Domino*, and what's more, the action was to be pushed back all the way to the 14th century. On this point Verdi was implacable. He was not opposed to transforming the king into a governor, or to relocating the action to a purely conventional America—in point of fact reduced to a mere reference in the libretto. But *Adelia* took place in an "epoch of iron and blood," whereas he had in mind an "elegant and chivalric century, such as that of Louis XIV and XV." This alone says a lot about Verdi's intentions as a dramatist, aside from the parenthesis of 1848 (which for Verdi, as for Wagner, must have gone by in the blink of an eye, such that we do not feel we need to accept Massimo Mila's reference to the politically reactionary character that he finds in this opera, making it a unique example in all of Verdi's theatrical works). Political events, whether a simple background to the action, as in *Ballo in Maschera*, or at the center of passions, as in *Don Carlo*, are always presented with objective detachment, immune to both documentary coolness and immediate emotional involvement, as is typical of classical authors. Returning to his investigation of passion, which his three popular operas had carried him far away from and which *Les Vêpres* had slowed, Verdi turned toward an area until then unexplored, beginning with a protagonist whom he wanted to be "amiable, brilliant, chivalrous," thus much different from the shameless vitality of the duke of Mantua. He had in fact been thinking of a "quiet, simple, tender drama," "a kind of

On these pages, two images of characters in *Un Ballo in Maschera*, Amelia (above) and Riccardo (opposite).

Sonnambula"—in reference to Bellini's opera—"without being an imitation," only to move from the idyllic into a new drama of jealousy, but one that differed from the old style because of the worldly setting, the slight foolishness of the protagonist, and the large-scale involvement of humor, which explodes in the role of the page and becomes, objectively, the moral counterpoint of the action, the vehicle for a kind of creativity and a fantasy not at all like that of Ariosto.

With the objections overcome, the decision was made to withdraw the opera from Naples and to give *Un Ballo in Maschera* to Rome. The premiere took place on February 17, 1859, at the Teatro Apollo, which had previously seen the creation of *Il Trovatore*, and it met with great success, even though the production was "partly good and partly very bad," in the estimation of Verdi himself.

Formally, Somma's text faithfully followed the play by Scribe, with marginal modifications. Even more than in the original, the politics of the sovereign were glossed over. Also, certain free-thinking comments that Scribe did not spare in terms of the magical arts of Ulrica were avoided. The scene before the tragic ball was amplified and made far more significant. Without doubt, the slightly frivolous levity of the page Oscar is drawn from the French theater. This Cherubino became more crafty than he had been in Paris, and the tone of frivolity, and almost of recklessness, taken from that environment is reflected on the protagonist, who displays amorous impulses that are not fully credible, with love accepted with the levity of an adventure, leading to the nonchalance of the fisherman's song with its "Mozartian ambiguity . . . which is at once joking fiction and arcane nostalgia" (D'Amico).

The French example (far more from the Opéra-Comique than the Opéra, and perhaps even more from vaudeville and operetta) inspired the incredible taste for agile, brilliant instrumentation and for rhythms that approach the adorable impudence of Offenbach (as in the close of the first scene). The French style is also in the presence, from beginning to end, of dance movements, hymns, and songs, including a mazurka rhythm that German experts call a *Todesmenuett* ("minuet of death"). Against a "tint" of this kind, such a refined background tone, the figure of Renato, with his dark jealousy, is starkly highlighted. This intrusion of a character typical of Verdi's drama into a context so transformed seems to make the psychological elements even more compelling. The role of the fortune-teller Ulrica, beginning with her character's admirable introduction ("Re dell'abisso"—"King of the abyss"), also stands out sharply against the golden Louis XIV background with bloody reflections.

This opera's unprecedented narrative capacity appears even in the "light" areas, which, the more they loosen their hold on the "too human," the better they sweep the story into a continuous whirlwind in which the force of destiny, or of chance, appears almost paradigmatically. Nowhere more than in this opera—which D'Annunzio acutely judged the most melodramatic of melodramas—does the play of chance prevail over the intentions and the wills of the characters. There are moments in which the "ironic" detachment is so explicit that the melodrama seems to come near declaring its rules, to turn itself into a meta-melodrama, or a metaphor for itself. A torrential inventiveness, above all melodic, keeps *Un Ballo in Maschera* from collapsing into the gratuitous, and that makes this perhaps the most outstanding instance of balance between poetry and poetics, between subconscious fertilization and rational

determination, in all of Verdi's works. In this work the characters and dramatic events are truly treated like playing cards, but without ever going far enough to reveal them as such, without letting the internal rhythm, the scansion of the events, dry up with the questionable intelligence of a disguised scheme, and it is enjoyed as such.

The opera is built on symmetries that are almost flaunted. Luigi Dallapiccola has shown this with the computation of beats in the central scene. But even without mathematical proofs, the correspondences between Acts I and III should be clear to anyone, with their two scenes of distinct character, around the central column of Act II. That act—in the depiction of nocturnal terror (scene and aria, "Ecco l'orrido campo"—"Here is the horrid field"), in the broad singability of the confession, in the excitement of the trio, and finally in the sublime scene of the "Laughing Chorus," with the effect of laughs that fade in the distance, digging channels of pain in the soul of the offended—reveals merciless premises resulting from the most fleeting freedom, since by now the music shines not so much "in a superior moral dialectic, which laughs at certain motivations," but because of an understanding of destiny, for which it yearns and of which it dares to repeat the delirious process; moral reasoning is but its pale counterfeit.

Thus *Un Ballo in Maschera* could even accommodate certain situations in Dumas's *Vicomte de Bragelonne*, or even touch on *feuilleton* stories (the oath of Act III), since, with its long experience, it has learned to read and decipher, depending on the circumstances, the mysterious laws behind them. [...]

Mario Bortolotto,
Guida all'Opera,
Arnoldo Mondadori Editore

La Forza del Destino

Melodramma in four acts to a libretto by Francesco Maria Piave, taken from the play *Don Alvaro, o La Fuerza del Sino* by Ángel de Saavedra, duke of Rivas, with one scene from the play *Wallensteins Lager* by Friedrich Schiller

FIRST PERFORMANCE
IMPERIAL THEATER, ST. PETERSBURG, NOVEMBER 10, 1862

FIRST PERFORMERS
CAROLINE BARBOT (LEONORA), CONSTANCE NANTIER-DIDIÉE (PREZIOSILLA),
ENRICO TAMBERLIK (ALVARO), FRANCESCO GRAZIANI (CARLO), ACHILLE DE BASSINI
(FRA MELITONE), GIAN FRANCESCO ANGELINI (PADRE GUARDIANO)

CHARACTERS

The marquis of
Calatrava (*bass*)
Donna Leonora, his
daughter (*soprano*)
Don Carlo di Vargas,
his son (*baritone*)
Don Alvaro (*tenor*)
Preziosilla, a young
gypsy (*mezzo-soprano*)
The Padre Guardiano,
a Franciscan (*bass*)
Fra Melitone, a Franciscan
(*baritone*)
Curra, Leonora's maid
(*mezzo-soprano*)
An alcalde (*bass*)
Mastro Trabuco, a muleteer,
then peddler (*tenor*)
A surgeon in the Spanish
army (*bass*)

CHORUSES AND EXTRAS
Spanish and Italian peasants,
Spanish and Italian soldiers,
Franciscan friars, poor
beggars, Spanish and Italian
vivandières, male and
female innkeepers, waiters,
muleteers, drummers,
tumblers, peddlers of all kinds

TIME: Around the mid-18th
century.
PLACE: Spain and Italy.

The final scene of Act II of
La Forza del Destino at the
Teatro alla Scala in Milan,
1965. Conducted by
Gianandrea Gavazzeni,
directed by Margherita
Wallmann. Principal per-
formers: the soprano Ilva
Ligabue, the tenor Carlo
Bergonzi, the baritone Piero
Cappuccilli, and the bass
Nicolai Ghiaurov.

PLOT

Act I

A room in the palace of the marquis of Calatrava in Seville. The marquis's daughter, Leonora, with the help of her maid Curra, is preparing to elope with her lover Don Alvaro, a Peruvian descendant from a royal line ferocious-ly hunted by the Spanish. Leonora is full of remorse concerning her father; when Don Alvaro arrives, he guesses at her state of mind and accuses her of not sharing his love. In response, Leonora abandons all hesitation. They are about

to flee when the marquis enters the room, sword in hand. Alvaro raises his pistol, but, to give himself up unarmed, tosses it to the floor; it goes off and mor-tally wounds the marquis, who before dying curses his daughter. The two unhappy lovers flee.

Act II

The large kitchen in a tavern in the village of Hornachuelos. Common people and muleteers chat and eat. Among them is Don Carlo, Leonora's brother; he has sworn to avenge his father's death and for quite a while has been on the trail of Alvaro and his sister, whom he believes ran off together. The truth, instead, is that since that tragic night the two have not seen each other, and Leonora, after spending a long time wandering, dis-guised in men's clothing, has now arrived at that same inn. Don Carlo has spotted the mysterious stranger and tries in vain to uncover his identity.

The scene shifts to the church and convent of the Madonna of the Angels. Leonora, still in male clothing, reaches the convent, where she hopes to seek asylum. To the Padre Guardiano (Father

Superior), she confides her afflictions and the desire to expiate her guilt in complete solitude. In vain the good father asks her to reflect; Leonora is unwilling to change her mind. In the end he gives in, rejoins the friars in the church, and makes them swear they will never violate for any reason the secret that surrounds the penitent; then he invokes on her the blessing of the Virgin. Leonora moves off toward the hermitage.

recognized each other and, indeed, become sincere friends after Alvaro saves Don Carlo's life in a brawl.

In the rooms of a superior officer. Don Alvaro, in the course of an extremely difficult battle, has been seriously wounded. Believing himself near death, he gives Don Carlo a key. He asks that after his death Don Carlo open a casket, remove the parcel he will find, and then burn it. Don Carlo swears he will do so, and the wounded man is carried into another room. In that moment a terrible suspicion enters Don Carlo: could that man be the murderer of his father and the seducer of his sister? He does not forget his vow, but opening the casket he finds a portrait of Leonora. A surgeon, meanwhile, announces that Alvaro is out of danger: Carlo, with ferocious joy, finally sees the hour of his revenge arrive.

A military camp. Night. Carlo meets Don Alvaro, who is wandering through the camp beset by sad thoughts. Don Carlo confronts him and, after making

Left, inset: The tenor Giuseppe Fancelli in the habit of Don Alvaro at Milan's La Scala.

Below, middle: *La Forza del Destino*, title page of the score, Edizioni Ricordi, 1869.

Below, bottom: Scene from the beginning of Act II, in the 1965 La Scala production, with sets and costumes by Nicola Benois.

Act III

Woods in the environs of Velletri, Italy. A fierce war is being fought between the imperial troops and the Spanish. Don Carlo and Don Alvaro, under false names, are fighting in the ranks of the French-Spanish army; they have not

himself known, challenges him to a duel. Alvaro tries in vain to lead his antagonist back to milder thoughts. From the excited words of Don Carlo, he understands that Leonora is alive but then, faced with the arrogance of the man, he draws his sword. Several soldiers separate the two adversaries. Carlo is dragged away, while Alvaro decides to withdraw to a convent and spend the rest of his life in prayer.

Act IV

Through a tragic twist of fate, Don Alvaro has taken the habit at the convent near which Leonora lives. Meanwhile, Carlo, still resolute in his desire for revenge, manages once again to find the place where Alvaro has sought refuge. The two are again face to face. Alvaro tries in vain to resist the provocations, but when Carlo contemptuously taunts

The bass Nicolai Ghiaurov (the Padre Guardiano) with soprano Montserrat Caballé (Leonora) in *La Forza del Destino* at La Scala in 1978. Conducted by Giuseppe Patanè, directed by Lamberto Puggelli, sets and costumes by Renato Guttuso and Paolo Bregni.

him, he unwillingly accepts the challenge to a duel to death.

Carlo and Alvaro battle near the cave where Leonora lives. Believing he will find a hermit, Alvaro rushes to Leonora seeking help for his wounded rival. With profound emotion Leonora and Alvaro recognize each other. Leonora runs to her brother, but an excruciating cry is heard; the dying

BACKGROUND AND ANALYSIS

We are now in January of 1861: for two years Verdi had not composed, believing his career as a composer to be over. "I hope I have bade farewell to the muses and that the temptation to pick up the pen again never returns to me," he wrote to Piave in September of 1859, a few months after the premiere of *Un Ballo in*

Left: Act III of *La Forza del Destino*, Teatro alla Scala, Milan, 1965–66 season. Directed by Margherita Wallmann, sets and costumes by Nicola Benois.

Below: Sketch by Scajoli for *La Forza del Destino*.

Carlo stabbed her when she leaned over him. Supported by the Padre Guardiano, Leonora returns to the scene. Alvaro breaks out in curses, but the Padre Guardiano asks him to repent. Leonora, before dying, invokes divine pardon for Alvaro. His mood brightened, and certain he will rejoin the woman he loves in heaven, Alvaro accepts with resignation the destiny that wants to keep him alive.

In the first version of the opera, after Leonora is mortally wounded by her brother, a tremendous storm begins to rage. The Padre Guardiano and other friars rush to her.

Meanwhile, Alvaro, at the height of desperation, runs to a cliff and yells, "Open, O earth, and swallow me, hell! Let the heavens fall and the human race perish," and hurls himself into a ravine. The friars kneel and implore divine mercy.

Maschera. Meanwhile, on August 29, in a small church in the Haute-Savoie, he married Giuseppina Strepponi. The next two years of his life were anything but restful: he traveled and worked the land, worked on enlargement of the villa of Sant'Agata, and was witness to great

Right: Verdi on a troika with some friends, St. Petersburg, 1862.

Below: View of St. Petersburg in a print from the second half of the 19th century.

prestigious both artistically and financially. As for the subject, after considering *Ruy Blas* by Victor Hugo, the choice fell on the drama *Don Álvaro, o La Fuerza del Sino* by Ángel de Saavedra, duke of Rivas. Verdi entrusted the libretto to Piave and was soon battling with him and tyrannizing him, asking and complaining about this or that verse, as had always been his habit. The opera was finally composed in the summer of

historical-political changes in Italy, which except for Venice and Rome was finally united as one.

Cavour, who along with Garibaldi was one of the principal architects of the national unification process, turned to Verdi to get him to join the first national parliament. Verdi tried every way he could to get out of it, but realized he couldn't refuse and gave in to the personal appeals from Cavour. Verdi was elected in the month of February and parted with Giuseppina for Turin, where, on February 18, 1861, the first Italian parliament assembled. Verdi remained there until the end of his term, in 1865.

At the same time a letter arrived from Russia from the tenor Enrico Tamberlik, who, in the name of the directors of the Imperial Theater, invited Verdi to write an opera for St. Petersburg. Verdi accepted. The offer was enormously

1861, and that November Verdi and Giuseppina left for Russia. They stayed three months, but the soprano got sick and the opera was not performed. The whole thing was rescheduled for the following autumn, in 1862.

Meanwhile, Verdi continued to work on the orchestration, and on November 10, *La Forza del Destino* (*The Force of Destiny*) finally had its premiere. Its reception was warm, nothing more. Several years went by, during which it was performed in theaters in Madrid, Rome, Reggio Emilia, New York, Vienna, and Buenos Aires, never once rousing particular enthusiasm. *La Forza* failed to take off, so Verdi, already greatly troubled about the finale, which, remaining faithful to Rivas, ended with Alvaro's suicide, decided to prepare variants. It seemed like the opera was already finished, but in reality it was not until 1869 that *La Forza* assumed its definitive form. The same period saw the equally difficult gestation of *Don Carlos*, which premiered in 1867. In addition, in December of that same year, poor Piave suffered paralysis that debilitated him, putting him in bed until his death, in 1876.

formulate a new ending inspired by Christian resignation. The finale was not the only change: the prelude became a sinfonia, the "Compagni" chorus was added to Act III, and all of the following duet of Alvaro and Carlo, which had closed the act in the St. Petersburg version, changed position: the act ended with the "Rataplan" chorus. There were also reworkings to the duet between Leonora and Alvaro (Act I), the duet between Leonora and the Padre Guardiano (Act II), the verses of Preziosilla (Act III), and the comic aria of Fra Melitone (Act III).

This new version of *La Forza del Destino* premiered at La Scala on February 27, 1869. Its success was nothing short of triumphant. Aside from reconciling Verdi with the Milanese theater, this "novel in music" brought to life by characters and situations so purposefully contrasting—in which the tragic

La Forza del Destino in a 1967 production at the Arena of Verona. Conducted by Franco Capuana, directed by Herbert Graf, sets and costumes by Attilio Colonello. Principal performers: the soprano Leyla Gencer, the tenor Gianfranco Cecchele, and the baritone Piero Cappuccilli.

Pressure was also on Verdi from Ricordi, who wanted to bring him back to the stage at La Scala, from which Verdi had been absent for more than twenty years. With the assistance of Antonio Ghislanzoni, Verdi managed to

and the comic move side by side, as do the religious and the humorous, the profane and the grotesque—was at last justly recognized as a masterpiece by Verdi, even if today it is an opera that divides fans from critics.

[...] The most striking characteristic of *La Forza del Destino* is the highly notable disproportion between the nucleus of dramatic action and the accessory episodes, the latter so numerous and important they give the opera a polycentric structure, disarticulated into a series of "scenes," each of which is not necessarily related to the others following a coherent or unitary line of development. Such a lack of coherence is usually interpreted as the imbalance typical of a transitional work, and such is what *La Forza* is unanimously judged to be, the work with which Verdi, having concluded the heroic period of his creative activity, began the search for a more elaborate and complex dramatic structure.

Against this structural lack of coherence, however, there is the substantial unity of the opera's musical invention, documented by Peter Várnai, who in a study on melody in *La Forza del Destino* demonstrated how it is derived in large part—especially in the roles of Leonora and Alvaro—from a single cell composed of an ascending interval of a sixth followed by a descent by degrees to the tonic or the dominant. For this reason Várnai called the form of *La Forza del Destino* a gigantic "theme with variations." Furthermore, corresponding to this coherence in the melodic invention is an equally solid harmonic coherence; in fact, the opera orbits around a tonal center of E. Most of the pieces are written in this key, major or minor, and that key naturally plays a preponderant role in the very numerous pieces in tonalities near G major, A major and minor, C-sharp minor, and B major and minor.

In our opinion, these observations corroborate the evocative hypothesis advanced by Gabriele Baldini (but unfortunately left in the state of a draft), according to which Verdi created with *La Forza del Destino* a kind of Russian opera *ante litteram*, and that therefore his "casual structure," composed of "multiple parallel musical and dramatic actions that are not presented at their decisive moment, but somewhat randomly, according to the needs of the dramatic-musical occasions"—this structure, far from representing the fruit of an unsuccessful attempt to amalgamate into a harmonic whole a clutter of heterogeneous elements, is instead the result of a prearranged design created to move toward a certain mindset held by the public for whom the opera was destined.

For our part, we would like to propose not to reevaluate but simply to review the position of what is without doubt the principal "defendant" in *La Forza del Destino*: Act III, and in particular the scene of the encampment, which is faulted, more than any other scene, for being a cumbersome and annoying appendage. And we would suggest a paradoxical operation: if one eliminates this finale, then the same must be done with any of the "spectacular" pieces in *Aida*, which is to say the opera that marks, according to a certain critical tradition, Verdi's first achievement of the new balance he'd sought in vain in *La Forza del Destino*. Thus one can imagine for a moment eliminating from *Aida* the finale of Act I or the exclusively "triumphalist" scenes of the finale of Act II, those pieces that clearly have an ornamental character but are nonetheless perfectly integrated in the well-designed mechanism of the action. According to us, this hypothetical amputation would not do great damage to *Aida*, whose special physiognomy would not come out of it substantially altered. On the other hand, a considerable emptiness would be created in *La Forza del Destino* with the risk of changing the nature of the highly particular character of this singular opera. For if we wanted to take our paradox to its extreme consequences, if one sought a focal center of this opera, it would be located exactly here, in the most eccentric place in terms of the thread of the story. It doesn't matter that the music played here is certainly almost always superficial, sometimes even decidedly unpleasant. With its total gratuitousness, in fact, the episode serves as an excellent example of the blind inexorability of the force of destiny that the title of the opera indicates as the work's true protagonist. With absolute scorn for even the least demand for credibility, Verdi plops down Preziosilla, Trabuco, and Melitone in the middle of that crowd of soldiers, recruits, beggars, and vivandières, every one of them extraneous. This total absurdity momentarily expands the meaning of these figures (and with them all of the crowd around them) beyond the borders of their variously believable characters to the point that they lose weight and corporeal substance and take on instead an exemplary value: this is no longer an encampment but rather—to use baroque terminology that does not ill suit the quality of the material, which still bears the imprint of its Spanish Counter-Reformation matrix—it is the "great theater of the world," in which poor human beings move about, constantly blown by the great wind of the irrational that dominates the stories of everyone (and what image could render that precarious nature more aptly than a military camp?). Even the encounter before this,

the "fatal certame" ("mortal combat") of Alvaro and Carlo, has as its background this theater, the lights of which reveal, retrospectively, the vanity of the illusion that induces the two antagonists to feel like actors and protagonists able to change the course of events with their actions, whereas in reality they are only instruments of a superior force that destines them to be both victim and killer, each of the other.

The only major figure missing from this sort of gathering of characters that Verdi assembles in Act III is Leonora. But Leonora occupies a singular position with respect to her companions in misfortune: she alone does not take long to understand the uselessness of struggling against the inescapable force above her. Alone, therefore, through the entire grim story, she never strikes but is always struck. However, in this conscious surrender to imperious, overwhelming fate, Leonora wins what is the only freedom possible for her: the awareness of her own existence, of her desolate condition of being a human creature. A helpless victim without escape, she sets herself above the destiny that tyrannizes her. In her surrender she finds the fullness of her humanity, which instead is obscured or even annulled in many victims just like her, who refuse to be aware of their condition. Thus Leonora is the most "successful" character in *La Forza del Destino*; she is indeed the only true character, while the others are, some more than others, mere "roles." Her figure is pulsating with true humanity and therefore is rich and full and vigorously individualized. [...]

Renato Di Benedetto,
Guida all'Opera,
Arnoldo Mondadori Editore

Some of the performers in the new version of *La Forza del Destino*, first presented at the Teatro alla Scala in Milan on February 27, 1869. The conductor was Eugenio Terziani (opposite, inset), and the cast included Teresa Stolz (Leonora; above), Ida Benza Nagy (Preziosilla; opposite, top left), Mario Tiberini (Alvaro), Luigi Colonnese (Carlo), Giacomo Rota (Fra Melitone), and Marcel Junca (Padre Guardiano; above, inset).

Don Carlos

Opera in five acts to a libretto by Joseph Méry
and Camille du Locle after the play *Don Carlos*
by Friedrich Schiller; Italian revised version by
Achille de Lauzières and Angelo Zanardini

FIRST PERFORMANCE AS *DON CARLOS*
THÉÂTRE DE L'OPÉRA, PARIS, MARCH 11, 1867
MARIE SASSE (ELISABETH), PAULINE GUÉYMARD-LAUTERS (EBOLI),
JEAN MORÈRE (DON CARLOS), JEAN-BAPTISTE FAURE (POSA),
LOUIS-HENRI OBIN (PHILIP II), JOSEPH DAVID (INQUISITOR)

FIRST PERFORMANCE OF THE ITALIAN REVISED VERSION IN FOUR ACTS
TEATRO ALLA SCALA, MILAN, JANUARY 10, 1884

FIRST PERFORMERS
ABIGAILLE BRUSCHI-CHIATTI (ELISABETTA), GIUSEPPINA PASQUA (EBOLI),
FRANCESCO TAMAGNO (DON CARLO), PAUL LHÉRIE (POSA),
ALESSANDRO SILVESTRI (FILIPPO II), FRANCESCO NAVARINI (INQUISITORE)

CHARACTERS

Philip II, king of Spain (*bass*)

Don Carlos, infante of Spain (*tenor*)

Rodrigue, marquis of Posa (*baritone*)

The Grand Inquisitor, blind, nonagenarian (*bass*)

Elisabeth of Valois (*soprano*)

Princess Eboli (*mezzo-soprano*)

Thibault, Elisabeth's page (*soprano*)

The countess of Aremberg (*silent*)

The count of Lerma (*tenor*)

An old monk (*bass*)

A royal herald (*tenor*)

Voice from heaven (*soprano*)

CHORUSES AND EXTRAS

Flemish deputies, inquisitors, lords and ladies of the Spanish court, populace, pages, guards of Philip II, monks, members of the Inquisition, soldiers, magistrates, deputies of the provinces of the Spanish empire

TIME: 1568.
PLACE: France and Spain.

Right: Don Carlos throws himself at the queen's feet in an unfinished sketch made for Schiller's play.

PLOT

Background Events

In 1566, Charles V of Spain abdicates and withdraws to the monastery of San Yuste. Philip II takes the throne and his son, Don Carlos, is engaged to Elisabeth of Valois, daughter of Henry II of France; to rush this marriage and end the war between France and Spain more quickly, Spanish envoys go to France.

Act I

The forest of Fontainebleau. Don Carlos, traveling incognito in the retinue of the Spanish ambassadors, sees Elisabeth for the first time and immediately falls in love. This joy is brief, however, for Henry II has decided to give Elisabeth in marriage to Philip II. Elisabeth, bound by reasons of state, feels obliged to accept. While cannons fire salutes and the people sing hymns to the return of peace, Elisabeth and Don Carlos express all their desperation.

Act II

Cloister of the of San Yuste monastery. Several monks pray at the tomb of Charles V. Here Don Carlos confides his sorrow to his friend Posa, who suggests he leave Spain and go to Flanders, where he is expected to make a gesture of peace. In the background, Philip and Elisabeth cross the cloister after praying at the tomb of Charles V. Again alone, Carlos and Posa swear eternal friendship.

Garden at the gates of the convent of San Yuste. A group of women await the queen, among them Princess Eboli. Elisabeth arrives, followed by Posa, who officially bears a letter from her mother, but in reality gives her a note in which Don Carlos expresses the desire to see

her again. After much hesitation, Elisabeth accepts and Posa leads Eboli and the other women away. Don Carlos enters and timidly asks Elisabeth for help getting the king to send him to Flanders. The conversation seems to end there, but their passion has been rekin-

Act III

The queen's gardens. Night. Don Carlos holds a message signed by a mysterious lady inviting him to a nocturnal meeting. He is convinced this must be Elisabeth, and great is his astonishment when he finds himself instead facing

Opposite, top: The American bass-baritone Simon Estes in the role of Philip II in *Don Carlo*, Teatro Comunale, Florence, 1985.

dled; Elisabeth, however, comes to her senses and harshly reproaches Don Carlos, who runs away in despair.

Suddenly Philip arrives. Angry because the queen has been left alone, he firmly dismisses the countess of Aremberg, the woman assigned to watch Elisabeth. When everyone else has left, the king detains Posa and invites him to request payment for the services he has rendered the crown. Posa urges compassion for the people of Flanders, and Philip, struck by his frankness, confides in him his anguish as a father and husband, begs him to watch his son Carlos and Elisabeth, and advises him to be wary of the Grand Inquisitor.

Princess Eboli, who is secretly in love with him. When the woman understands his true feelings, she swears to get revenge. Posa intervenes to defend Carlos, and when Eboli leaves he asks Carlos to give him all the compromising letters he carries with him. Carlos is briefly in doubt, but then, trusting his friend, he gives him the letters.

In the great cathedral square of Valladolid, an auto-da-fé is being celebrated. From one side of the square several Flemish deputies advance, led by Carlos, and they ask for clemency and peace for Flanders. When the king refuses to listen to them, Carlos rushes at him with his sword, but he is stopped by Posa.

Don Carlo and Posa in the prison scene (Act IV), here performed by the tenor Michael Sylvester and the baritone Alexandru Agache. Teatro La Fenice, Venice, 1991.

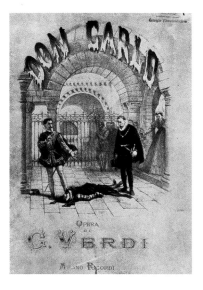

Right: Period title page of the piano-vocal score of *Don Carlo*, with the title dripping blood.

Below: Act V of *Don Carlo* in the Venetian production of 1991. The performers included the soprano Daniela Dessì (Elisabetta), the soprano Giovanna Casolla (Eboli), and the bass Samuel Ramey (Filippo II). Conducted by Daniel Oren, directed by Mauro Bolognini, sets by Mario Ceroli and Gianfranco Fini, costumes by Piero Tosi.

Act IV

The king's study. It is nearly dawn, and Philip II, absorbed in sad thoughts, sees that his life has been a failure, leaving him without love and without any more ideals. The Grand Inquisitor is introduced: blind and very old, he is supported by two monks. The king has summoned him to get an answer to the many problems that beset him, not the least of which is the fate of Carlos. The Inquisitor responds by reminding him that God sacrificed *his* son; but there is another problem, the Inquisitor says, that is even more serious: the marquis of Posa must be handed over to the Inquisition. At first Philip refuses, but when he is threatened with undergoing judgment himself, he gives in. The Inquisitor leaves.

At this point the queen comes in, highly agitated because someone has stolen the casket with her most precious mementoes. The king coldly shows her

the casket, pulls out a portrait of Don Carlos, and accuses her of adultery. Elisabeth faints. Princess Eboli rushes in and repents; she confesses her sins (she stole the casket and became the king's mistress) and decides to retire to a convent.

Meanwhile, in the prison where Don Carlos is being held, Posa announces to him that he will not be condemned: to save him, Posa has accused himself, using the documents Carlos entrusted to him. Carlos doesn't believe his friend, but suddenly an assassin's arquebus shot strikes Posa and kills him. While the king goes to free his son, the people sing a hymn to Don Carlos.

Act V

The monastery of San Yuste. In the cloister Elisabeth prays at the tomb of

BACKGROUND AND ANALYSIS

After 1862, the year of the first performance of *La Forza del Destino* in St. Petersburg, Verdi frequently undertook trips abroad. He seemed especially eager to do his work outside Italy. For a long time he'd been unhappy with the national theaters, not to mention the censors. From *La Traviata* to *Un Ballo in Maschera* the problems had outweighed the satisfactions. It seemed better to take some time out and work abroad, in particular for the Opéra in Paris, an opulent theater that offered a stable company and high-level choruses and orchestras. There he could also depend on the highest standard of stagings. Of course, there were negative points, such as the extremely bureaucratic management of

Charles V for the protection of Don Carlos. He himself arrives to give her a final farewell: he is going to Flanders to defend the ideals of liberty. Philip II and the Grand Inquisitor burst onto the scene, seeing the pair as guilty lovers. Don Carlos is about to be arrested when the tomb of Charles V opens wide and, amid general dismay, an old monk appears wrapped in the imperial cloak and drags off the amazed Don Carlos, taking him into the tomb.

the Opéra's "machine," which resulted in endless, exhausting discussions of each problem. That was the aspect Verdi disliked the most.

The offer to set Schiller's *Don Carlos* to music reached Verdi during a visit to Paris to discuss a reworking of *La Forza del Destino*. He and the management never managed to reach an agreement on *La Forza*, but they aimed at creating a new work for the 1867 Exposition. During the search for a subject to set to

The second scene in Act II, the garden outside the San Yuste monastery, in a production of the Teatro Comunale, Florence, 1985. Conducted by James Conlon; direction, sets, and costumes by Pier Luigi Pizzi.

music, Léon Escudier, Verdi's French publisher, proposed several works, including *Re Lear* and a sketch of a drama of *Don Carlos*, written by Joseph Méry and Camille du Locle. Perhaps weary of thinking of *Re Lear* for so long, Verdi discarded it, repeating his judgment on *Lear*: "A magnificent drama, but one that perhaps lacks a little of the spectacular." Verdi concentrated instead on *Don Carlos*, which presented a true challenge to him. Méry had died before

The Bulgarian bass Boris Christoff, one of the most acclaimed interpreters of the role of Filippo II.

completing his libretto, and the work had been continued by du Locle. The final work differed in several ways from Schiller's play: the act at Fontainebleau and the scene of the auto-da-fé did not exist in Schiller. It was anyway necessary to move away from the historical reality. Verdi himself wrote, "Posa is an imaginary being who could never have existed under Philip's reign," and of the entire drama he said, "In the end there is nothing historical in this drama, but there is Shakespearean truth and profundity in the characters." In confirmation of this Verdi added, "To copy the truth can be a good thing, but *to invent the truth* is better, much better."

The writing was difficult and involved continuous changes to this opera, which doubtless represents the *summa* of one of the aspects of drama dearest to Verdi: the conflict between an individual's public duty and his human passions, with the sacrifice of those passions to honor. All the characters—Carlos, Philip, Elisabeth, Posa, and Eboli—are closely and indissolubly tied one to the next, and so the drama of one character influences all the others in a chain reaction, but their actions also affect the community as a whole.

On the eve of the Paris premiere of *Don Carlos*, the work had reached such truly titanic proportions that it exceeded the maximum time permitted at the Opéra, which was saying something in a theater used to the "grand opera" of Meyerbeer. Verdi immediately began making cuts, in particular reworking the part of the protagonist, most of all because the singer, the tenor Morère, was not in a perfect vocal state. *Don Carlos* finally premiered on the evening of March 11, 1867, and met with somewhat modest success. The unhappy Verdi immediately left for Sant'Agata to deal with various family problems, including the recent death of his father. Verdi said this of the Paris premiere: "Last night *Don Carlos*. It was not a success! I don't know what will happen in the future, and I wouldn't be surprised if things changed." And then: "At the Opéra you do eight months of rehearsals and end up with an execution that is bloodless and cold."

A few months after the Parisian premiere, on October 26, 1867, *Don Carlos*, transformed into the Italian *Don Carlo*, but with the same composition as the French version, was performed in Bologna, conducted by Angelo Mariani. This time it met with great success. This was also the opinion at La Scala the next year, on March 25, 1868. Verdi undertook further reworking slowly and made continuous adjustments: adhering to the drama of Schiller's work was always of great importance to him. In 1872, using verses by Antonio Ghislanzoni, he changed one of the fundamental moments in the opera, the duet between the marquis of Posa and Philip II.

Ten years later, while Verdi and Boito were busy working on *Otello*, Verdi was persuaded to redo *Don Carlos* for a performance in Vienna. This Viennese revival did not take place, but as Verdi wrote to a friend, "Operas that are too long are savagely amputated": he eliminated the Fontainebleau act, except for Carlos's only aria, the ballet, and the preceding scene in which Elisabeth and Eboli exchange clothes, thus making clearer the error of Carlos. He

also cut back the riot scene in Act IV. Such were the clearest elements of the *Don Carlo* performed at La Scala on January 10, 1884. Two years later, however, Verdi himself consented to the performance, in Modena, of a version that reintegrated Act I as well as to the publication of this version, combining Act I with the other four acts as revised in the version of 1884. Even later, Verdi gave permission to perform the first part of Act III (the part with the ballet) from the Parisian version. This was part of Verdi's dual nature: on the one hand, in order to safeguard his creations, he insisted that his works should always be performed the way he had written them; on the other hand, he himself made changes to vocal parts, cuts, adaptations, and rewrites.

Don Carlo(s) thus seems like it was destined to be an opera "in progress."

The soprano Giovanna Casolla, a convincing interpreter of the role of Eboli, here in a production at the Metropolitan Opera in New York.

The grand scene of the auto-da-fé in Act III of *Don Carlo* at the Teatro alla Scala in Milan, in the spectacular inauguration of the 1992–93 season. At the center is the soprano Daniela Dessì (Elisabetta) and the bass Samuel Ramey (Filippo II). Conducted by Riccardo Muti, direction and sets by Franco Zeffirelli, costumes by Anna Anni.

[. . .] The reassessment of *Don Carlo* is recent history. For a long time it was considered a transitional work, composite and uneven, influenced by the conventions of fashionable melodrama, those that were imposed by the Paris Opéra. Today, such observations, somewhat superficial and imprecise, must be suitably reworked, if not overturned. And this should certainly not be done in an equally simplistic way by negating the weight of that influence with the basically obvious observation that Verdi always remained Verdi and did not in any way give in to the different demands of melodrama.

In reality that juxatposition did exist and was determinant. That Verdi wanted to pay some tribute to French taste and to the cultural level of Second Empire France is uncontestable. But rather than causing a regression, that involvement resulted in a profitable turn in Verdi's creative process, an unimaginable enrichment and an inspired provocation. Only rarely did Verdi give in to Parisian "facility": in Princess Eboli's "Song of the Veil," for example, which reproposes the exotic enticements of a faux Spanish style, according to a commonplace typical of French culture—one need only think of Daniel Auber's opera *Fra Diavolo*—that endured up until Bizet and Ravel. But otherwise, indeed in most cases, the juxtaposition proved beneficial, in part because Verdi was capable of giving the machinery of the "grand opéra" a grandly funerary patina. The orchestral writing, for example, throughout the entire opera has an exceptional prominence that sounds absolutely new for Verdi.

When the opera was first performed, in 1867, there were those who took Verdi to task for giving in to Wagnerian fever. In reality, the orchestration showed the influence of trends in European music, but the filter, rather than being Germany, was Paris. Naturally, Verdi greatly outdid his models and fashioned for himself a made-to-measure outfit. It is not at all daring to suggest that in terms of its instrumentation *Don Carlo* may well constitute Verdi's most resounding success. It has an especially differentiated and analytical orchestration, capable of subtleties until then unforeseeable from the author of *Il Trovatore*. There is, for example, the instrumental coloring of the prelude to the garden scene in Madrid, which is midway between the intimate nocturne of Act III of *Aida* and *Lohengrin*. Although the hypothesis may seem daring, one passage even sounds like a precursor of Mahler; the ghostly fanfare that plays at the moment of the killing of the marquis of Posa has a similarly powerful sense of poignant evocation.

This opera, more than any other of Verdi's, including the last two, shows signs of certain ferments in European thought from the close of the century, and the music's essential role is to improve the psychological insight of the libretto—already so clear in the Schiller play it was based on—and to help it acquire further, sharper clarity. The six major characters in this vast story (these being, aside from the protagonist, Filippo II, the Grand Inquisitor, the marquis of Posa, Elisabetta, and

A pleasant spot near the doors to the convent of San Yuste. Sketch by Edoardo Marchioro for *Don Carlo*, second scene of Act II, Teatro alla Scala, Milan, 1926.

Princess Eboli) receive, as was habitual in Verdi's vocalism, an individualization based essentially on the resources of each performer's tessitura and secondarily, but certainly not marginally, on a vocal invention of the highest perspicuity. All told, it is as if the author managed to think of the traditional art of Italian singing in at least six possible interpretations. The usual border between recitative and aria, already greatly softened in the earlier popular masterpieces with the large-scale application of a dramatic arioso style, is here practically dissolved in the vivid reality of a melodic plasticity that runs uninterrupted for the full length of the long score. The success of this opera was impaired by its dark subject and a certain immobility of action, and perhaps also the excessive length Verdi indulged in to comply with the customs of the French lyric theater. Elisabetta's fatal, unstoppable love for Don Carlo; Filippo II's sense of inferiority, not unrelated to jealousy, regarding the youth of his son; Princess Eboli's blind passion; and the profound attraction that drives Carlo to the young woman were the leading incentives behind Verdi's inspiration, which this time had its anonymous background in the austere, gloomy atmosphere of the Spanish court. In the effort to musically—and above all, vocally—characterize such an inextricable tangle of situations, in Don Carlo the melodies no longer stand out against a sharp design, simple and incisive, as in so many of the earlier operas, for the vocalism is often accompanied by an effort that could be called instrumental, and the arias most of all are no longer as well-defined and plastic as they were in *Il Trovatore* and *La Traviata*.

With regard to the vocal characterizations, special attention must be given those places where the homogeneity of the medium might seem to block it.

Outstanding in this regard is the famous duet between Filippo II and the Grand Inquisitor, two roles that are both entrusted to basses. It seems very probable that the idea may have come to Verdi from his study of the scene of the tragic banquet in Mozart's *Don Giovanni*. Also in this instance, in the search for differentiation by affinity instead of by elementary contrasts, Verdi showed a surprising enlargement of his thinking on the act of musical composition. Furthermore that adoption of a harmonic language capable of accepting all of what contemporary chromaticism had experienced allows us to consider this opera as a point of arrival in the history of Verdi's drama. It is a drama that still confronts, and with an awareness very different than was customary, the problem of royalty. Earlier, Verdi, too, had given in more than a little to a facile and old-fashioned populism; now royalty was viewed on one hand as a normative fact and on the other as an occasion for criticism. But this highly singular psychological implication is not defined only on the vocal plane; it is also embodied in a highly agile orchestra that from time to time emphasizes the apprehensions and the ambiguities of Filippo II with mysterious reverberations, echoes of a lost greatness. The other focal center is the impossible love of Don Carlo and Elisabetta, which is endowed with long and continually changing expansions, all held on a flexible melodic line (with another echo of the French in the luxuriance of the tenor's aria). [...]

Mario Messinis,
Guida all'Opera,
Arnoldo Mondadori Editore

The famous French tenor Jean Morère, interpreter of the title role at the premiere of *Don Carlos* at the Opéra in Paris on March 11, 1867, in a period photo.

Aida

Melodramma in four acts to a libretto by
Antonio Ghislanzoni, from Camille du Locle
and Auguste Mariette

FIRST PERFORMANCE
THEATER OF THE OPERA, CAIRO, DECEMBER 24, 1871

FIRST PERFORMERS
ANTONIETTA ANASTASI-POZZONI (AIDA), ELEONORA GROSSI (AMNERIS),
PIETRO MONGINI (RADAMES), FRANCESCO STELLER (AMONASRO),
PAOLO MEDINI (RAMFIS), TOMMASO COSTA (THE KING)

CHARACTERS

The king of Egypt (*bass*)
Amneris, his daughter
(*mezzo-soprano*)
Aida, an Ethiopian slave
(*soprano*)
Radames, captain of the
guard (*tenor*)
Ramfis, chief priest (*bass*)
Amonasro, king of Ethiopia,
father of Aida (*baritone*)
A messenger (*tenor*)
A priestess (*soprano*)

CHORUSES AND EXTRAS
Priests, priestesses,
ministers, captains, soldiers,
functionaries, Ethiopian
slaves and prisoners,
Egyptian people

TIME: The age of the
pharaohs.
PLACE: Ancient Egypt, at
Memphis and Thebes.

PLOT

Act I

Royal palace at Memphis. The chief priest Ramfis tells Radames that the Ethiopians are threatening war against Egypt and that the goddess Isis has chosen the one who will lead the Egyptian army against the invader. Radames hopes to be chosen so he can return victorious to Aida, the Ethiopian slave he loves. But the pharaoh's daughter, Amneris, is also

infatuated with him. The princess, noticing Radames's embarrassed response when Aida appears, realizes the slave is a rival. Meanwhile, the king arrives and a messenger announces that Amonasro has entered Egypt with his army. This means war! The pharaoh reveals the supreme commander: Radames. The crowd exults and invokes victory for the Egyptians. Left alone,

Aida is tormented by agony because she loves the man who will lead the army against her father and her people.

The scene changes to the temple of the god Vulcan. Ramfis prays together with the priests and priestesses. The priestesses perform a sacred dance as Radames dons the sacred armor. Then Ramfis hands him the sacred sword.

Act II

Room in Amneris's apartments in Thebes. The princess is preparing to celebrate Radames's victory over the Ethiopians. Alone with Aida, Amneris manages with simulated tenderness and underhanded approaches to make her reveal her love for Radames. At that point, full of disdain, she proclaims herself Aida's rival and orders the slave to follow her to the celebrations of the triumph.

Outside the walls of Thebes. The people and the court welcome the victor Radames, who in front of the pharaoh

Near right: Poster for the 1913 production of *Aida* that began the operatic activity of the Arena di Verona and marked the centennial of Verdi's birth.

orders the Ethiopian prisoners to be brought forward. Among them is Amonasro, Aida's father. Hiding his identity as king, he tells the pharaoh that Amonasro was killed in battle and therefore asks for freedom and clemency for the Ethiopians. Ramfis and the priests are opposed, but in the end they give in, provided that Aida and her father remain in Egypt as hostages. The king approves and announces his desire to give the hand of Amneris to Radames. Amid the general cries of delight, Aida and Radames have difficulty hiding their desperation.

Act III

Temple of Isis near the banks of the Nile. On the eve of her wedding to Radames, Amneris, accompanied by Ramfis, goes to the temple of the goddess to invoke her blessing. A little later Aida arrives. She is awaiting Radames, but is joined instead by Amonasro, who is aware of her feelings for the Egyptian and orders her to find out the Egyptian war plans. Aida at first refuses but then, fearing her father's wrath, gives in. Amonasro hides among the palms.

Radames finally arrives and promises Aida that after his campaign against the Ethiopians, he will ask the pharaoh for her hand. Aida does not believe him, fearing Amneris's anger, and convinces Radames to leave Egypt forever. She then asks him by which route they can flee and avoid the Egyptian sentries. "The gorges of Napata," he says. Amonasro has heard all this and now reveals his true identity. Radames is briefly at a loss but then

Inset: The tenor Giovanni Zenatello in costume as Radames in an historical photograph. In 1913 Zenatello inaugurated the opera season in the Arena di Verona, which was a result of his initiative; he was later its impresario for several years.

The great triumphal scene in Act II of *Aida* in a production at the Teatro La Fenice in Venice in 1984. Conducted by Eliahu Inbal, directed by Mauro Bolognini, sets by Mario Ceroli, costumes by Aldo Buti.

realizes he has betrayed his own people. Surprised by Amneris and Ramfis, Amonasro pounces on Amneris to kill her, but Radames stops him. Aida and her father manage to flee into the night while Radames surrenders to Ramfis.

Act IV

Hall of the royal palace. Amneris seeks a way to save Radames from certain condemnation. She has the prisoner brought to her and promises him to intercede on his behalf, provided he gives up Aida. Radames accuses her of killing his beloved. No, Aida is alive, Amneris responds, only Amonasro is dead, killed by the pursuers. Reassured of the fate of Aida, Radames refuses all help and shows himself ready to pay with his life for his treason. Led to judgment, he does not defend himself, and Amneris listens with anguish to the terrible sentence: he is condemned to be buried alive. In vain she seeks to oppose this and curses the cruelty of Ramfis and his priests.

The final scene is divided in two levels: the upper one shows the interior of the temple, the lower an underground darkness. Radames has just entered what will become his tomb. He is startled to see a human figure: it is Aida. Having returned in secret to Memphis, she has managed to enter the underground space to die with him. The two await the liberation of death while in the temple above sound the choruses of the priests and the prayer of Amneris, who implores eternal peace for the man she loves.

Above: The Aida/Amneris duet in Act II of the opera, here performed by the soprano Natalia Troitskaya and the mezzo-soprano Gail Gilmore, Teatro La Fenice, Venice, 1984.

Right: The report of the messenger (Manuel Ferri, tenor) in Act I of *Aida*. Teatro La Fenice, Venice, 1984.

BACKGROUND AND ANALYSIS

Immediately after the Parisian premiere of *Don Carlos* in March of 1867, the greatly disillusioned Verdi returned to Sant'Agata. This was an especially difficult period for the fifty-three-year-old composer. While in Paris he'd received news of the death of his father, and now, in the quiet of the countryside, he was present at the death of Antonio Barezzi, the father of his first wife, Margherita, as well as a friend and benefactor. Saddened by the death of the man who had remained close through every step of his career, Verdi was again upset to learn that his old and much-mistreated collaborator Francesco Maria Piave had been struck by a malady that left him paralyzed and unable to speak. The unfortunate Piave was destined to remain in that sad state for eight years, while Verdi provided financial support to his family.

Yet another hard blow struck Verdi in November of the following year, when Gioachino Rossini died in Paris. Verdi tried to put together a committee of musicians to compose a Requiem Mass to be performed on the first anniversary of Rossini's death, but organizational difficulties made them miss the date for the performance of this monumental score. The "Libera me Domine," the section assigned to Verdi, remained, and he reused it in his *Messa da Requiem* in 1874.

Verdi was not busy with new subjects in this period; he closely followed the performance of the revised *Forza del Destino* (February 1869) and continued work on *Don Carlos*. Camille du Locle, the librettist of that opera, meanwhile, continued to suggest subjects and tried to convince him to return to Paris. But Verdi was categorical: "I am not a composer for Paris. I do not know if I have the talent, but I do know that my ideas

Verdi at the podium of the Opéra conducting the Paris premiere of *Aida*, March 22, 1880.

in matters of art are quite different from yours. I believe in inspiration, you in workmanship."

Du Locle did not give up and continued his efforts at persuasion, succeeding at last in calling Verdi's attention to a subject set in ancient Egypt, drawn from a story by the French Egyptologist Auguste Mariette. Raised to the rank of bey by the khedive of Egypt, Mariette proposed this subject for an opera that would be used to celebrate the opening

The great concertato in Act II of *Aida*, in the sumptuous La Scala production of 1963. Conducted by Gianandrea Gavazzeni, directed by Franco Zeffirelli, sets and costumes by Lila De Nobili. Principal performers: the soprano Leontyne Price, the mezzo-soprano Fiorenza Cossotto, and the tenor Carlo Bergonzi.

Aida. Atto IV.

of the Suez Canal. This was somewhat illogical, since Verdi received the plot of the opera in the spring of 1870; the Suez Canal had been opened in October 1869. All this aside, Verdi agreed to write the opera that became *Aida*, but he did not accept the libretto as completed by du Locle, since he had no intention of composing in French; for the Italian version he engaged Antonio Ghislanzoni, with whom he'd already worked on the revision of *La Forza del Destino*.

the opera, which took place at the Teatro alla Scala on February 8, 1872.

In *Aida* Verdi presents the basic elements of his theatrical drama: the oppression of one people by another, and the irreconcilability of human passions with the demands of state, the good of the community. The parallels with *Don Carlos* are fairly clear: in *Don Carlos* the power controlling the actions of the individuals is the Grand Inquisitor; here we have Ramfis, another priestly figure,

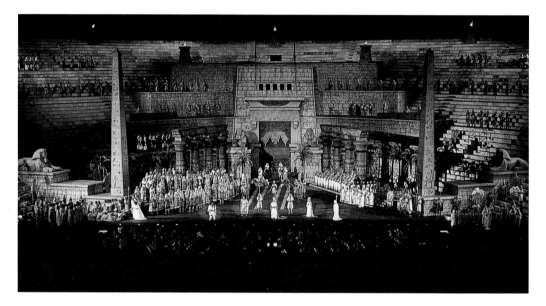

Above, top: A typical postcard of the period, designed to celebrate the splendor and the success of Verdi's operas.

Above, middle: The scene of the triumph of Radames in the Arena di Verona, in the 1982 reconstruction of the first production of the opera at the amphitheater, in 1913. This 1982 stage design was repeated in many later seasons.

With his pliant personality—a must for working with Verdi—Ghislanzoni wrote the libretto under Verdi's continuous control. The premiere, planned for Cairo's Theater of the Opera in January of 1871, had to be put off eleven months because of events related to the Franco-Prussian War: "My opera for Cairo is finished, but it can't be performed because the costumes and sets are still locked up in Paris. Just as well! But this horrible war is serious."

Aida was performed with success on the evening of December 24, 1871. Verdi was not present, having remained in Italy to prepare the Italian premiere of

who manipulates the fortunes of the main characters in ways that are more or less hidden. So just as Philip II cannot save Posa from the condemnation of the Grand Inquisitor, Amneris is impotent against Ramfis, who has "created" Radames and now destroys him.

In their triumphalism, the great scenes of the auto-da-fé and the triumph make clear the image of power that is nevertheless illusory, even as it oppresses the individual and the community—"illusory" because the true power is far less visible, but in reality is shown through the ostentation of the other power. Ramfis, compared to the Grand Inquisitor, is an even more threatening figure, more openly manipulating the actions and the situations of other people. It is no accident that the figure of the pharaoh is almost nonexistent.

From the musical point of view, beyond the spectacular aspects, which are certainly the most striking, what emerges in this work is Verdi's effort to recreate the evocative colors of a lost and distant world. Verdi put great care into the presentation of *Aida*, but it is in the orchestral color that the most fascinating

aspects of this opera appear. Verdi succeeded in inventing sounds that convey a suggestion of the oriental. Thus, on the one hand, Egyptian power is evoked by the sound of six trumpets, three in A-flat and three in B-natural—the long, straight "Aida trumpets" Verdi himself invented, inspired by ancient bas-reliefs. On the other hand, there is the exotic, verdant, sensual world of Aida, evoked by the clarinet, with its supple melody making that is, however, distant and thus what

Below, center: The soprano Montserrat Caballé (Aida), the mezzo-soprano Grace Bumbry (Amneris), and the tenor Carlo Bergonzi (Radames) in Act I of *Aida* in a 1976 revival of the 1963 Zeffirelli/De Nobili production at La Scala.

ANTONIO GHISLANZONI

Antonio Ghislanzoni (1824–1893) was born in Lecco, in Lombardy, son of a doctor who had accompanied Napoleon during several campaigns. "As a young boy I was started out on an ecclesiastical career for which I felt no calling. I then studied medicine at the University of Pavia. In 1848 I threw myself into the revolutionary scuffles; when Lombardy fell under Austrian domination, I set off for Rome to take part in the defense of that patch of the republic and fell into the power of the French soldiers besieging the city. ... When I was again free, I thought about profiting from my beautiful baritone voice and my knowledge of music to make a living."

His operatic career was cut short by bouts of poorly treated bronchitis. Meanwhile, he dedicated himself fully to writing and made a name for himself as an authoritative literary critic, showing a great openness to

new trends in poetry. At the same time, however, as music critic of Milan's Società del Quartetto he showed himself to be quite conservative, taking a firm stance in regard to Wagner and his followers. His encounter with Verdi was of fundamental importance to his career as a librettist. After reworking the finale of La Forza del Destino *in the 1869* La Scala *version, with* Aida *(1871) he earned great fame as well as great earnings. From then on he was one of the most sought-after librettists (he was to write more than eighty librettos). Aside from* Aida, *his most outstanding works include the libretto for* I Promessi Sposi *by Errico Petrella, staged in Lecco in 1869 with enormous success. Another great success was* I Lituani *(1874) by Amilcare Ponchielli, based on the historical poem* Konrad Wallenrod *by Adam Mickiewicz.*

we might call a "melody of memory." So even the music does not fail to highlight the contrasts between the two worlds: the Egyptian, closed in rigid rituality, and the Ethiopian, dynamic but experienced through nostalgia.

Above, inset: The librettist Antonio Ghislanzoni, who wrote for Verdi the libretto of *Aida* and the new version of *La Forza del Destino*.

[…] In composing *Aida* Verdi kept in mind the theatrical demands of "grand opéra," but if we had to say in brief what the aesthetic result of this labor was, we would find it in its own extreme variety of attitudes. For while *Aida* has become popular because of some of its explosive musical scenes, few other operas by the mature Verdi have such an intimate and polished finesse in their psychological undertones. And what is striking is precisely this surprising ability of Verdi to smoothly transition—in complete theatrical "truth"—from large group passages to the inner solitude of the principal characters (in particular Aida, Amneris, and Amonasro), finding an intangible connective fabric—

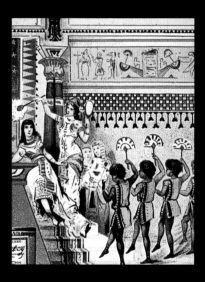

One of many popular prints of *Aida* made to commemorate its triumphant performance in Paris in 1880.

which in fact struck the first listeners and the first critics and often misled their judgment—in the presence of an "exoticism" that could be considered an invisible but ever-present "new" character.

After the prelude, which already prefigures the intimist and tragic dimensions of the opera, the introduction and the famous romanza of Radames ("Celeste Aida"—"Heavenly Aida") seem to get us back in touch with a popular and essential Verdi and have a more popular than emotional value. But the next duet, with Aida and Amneris, and the trio of the two women with Radames touch instead the first dramatic high points of the opera. A truly "indomitable" orchestra establishes a continuous dynamic relationship, masterfully graded in its tension and in the choice of timbres, as though to prearrange the moving contrast of that *allegro giusto poco agitato* that precedes the blossoming of Aida's "Numi, pietà" ("Gods, have pity"), among the greatest passages by Verdi.

The scene of the consecration and the finale of Act I bring us back to the demands of "grand opéra," but even here the landscape "invented" by Verdi colors the orchestra (harmonically and timbrally) with an unusual and seductive color, the same one—more "impressionistic," as we might call it—that we find in the introduction of Act II up to the "Dance of the Young Moorish Slaves."

There is vigorous drama in the scene of Aida and Amneris: from the hypocritical insinuation, to furor, and from sorrow to pity, the compositional arc seems again to calm in the reappearance of Aida's "Numi, pietà," suddenly shattered by the grand finale of Act II, with the hymn, the triumphal march, and the dances. Also on this occasion the *ballabili* (dance pieces) have a particular symphonic quality, for the breadth and the variety of their "exotic" insertions. But the ensemble piece that concludes the act brings back the "heroic" and popular Verdi: the relationship between orchestra and stage becomes positively feverish, and not immune to certain rhetorical concessions, ending with a repeat of the triumphal theme.

Act III, so intentionally "aquatic" in its initial impressionistic design (the color that the flute takes here is among the most evocative timbral effects by Verdi), has a progression—and, we might say, a depth—of particular homogeneity. The alternation of intimist moments with those more of a "landscape," more apparent here than anywhere else, make this perhaps the most successful act of the entire opera. The Aida/Amonasro duet represents one of the most beautiful pairings by Verdi, and the *andante assai sostenuto* that introduces the "Pensa che un popolo, vinto" ("Remember that a people, conquered") of the baritone (kept *pianissimo* with the climax barely a cry) prepares for the scene between Aida and Radames, in which Radames acquires greater dramatic and psychological importance while holding himself dangerously in the balance, at risk of falling into a certain "tenorism" of effects, confirmed in the finale of the act.

Act IV displays extraordinary musical fineness in the highly measured manipulation of several leitmotifs of Amneris: the grandeur of the representative structure and, all things considered, the ingenuity of the proposals of the enamored princess translate into a drama that does not suffocate, but instead enhances, a vast fabric of cries and sobs. Even the "Chi ti salva, sciagurato" ("Who will save you, wretch"; *allegro agitato*) has a strophic progression almost like a cabaletta that adheres to the situation with great felicity, almost as if Verdi meant to accentuate the bloody tone of this scene to augment the sense of catharsis in the judgment scene. The "local color" reappears here, but tinged—as has been observed—by an open aversion to the "sacred" judges, almost overturning the image of all the earlier sumptuous scenes ("Oh, the villains! They can never have enough blood. And the call themselves ministers of heaven!" Amneris yells). Verdi presents the finale of the opera with a certain intentionality: the transparency of the instrumentation, the breadth of the timbral weave, the struggle to free the tenor (finally) from the weight of his warrior's

entire scene a theatrical sheen, even if it can't be considered among Verdi's most felicitous passages.

The accusation of "Wagnerism," in various shadings, has accompanied the path of this opera for quite some time. Verdi's admirers have responded to the charge in horrified tones. But it cannot be denied that Verdi sensed something in the air was changing, and with his usual genius he made many of his own new experimentations (as we would call them today) of harmonic and orchestral nature, moving forward on a path almost parallel to Wagner's. Thus the critic Eduard Hanslick, in his *Die Moderne Oper*, affirmed that "in *Aida* there is not a beat for which the Italian is indebted to the German." He added, "The entire composition of *Aida* is dominated, like an invisible church, by the law of drama, but its visible leader forever remains musical beauty."

Among 20th-century critics, Massimo Mila affirmed that *Aida* "is difficult to defend precisely on the terrain of its greatest success, the opulent processions, the triumphal marches, and the gleaming lights; but it then redeems itself in the most unforeseeable manner, on the terrain of 'dramatic conscientiousness', of 'diligence in technical elaboration', and most of all in the 'nobility and unity of style' that Hanslick rightly admired." To Andrea Della Corte, the character of Radames "is completely inconsistent," and the greatest merits of the opera "rich in imagination and full of music in every part" are in the dramatic power of Amonasro and Aida. [...]

Leonardo Pinzauti,
Guida all'Opera,
Arnoldo Mondadori Editore

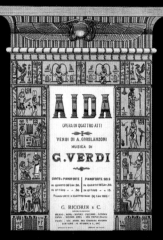

Cover of the score of *Aida*. The opera has always enjoyed great popularity and has been presented in many piano-solo reductions and scores for voice and piano.

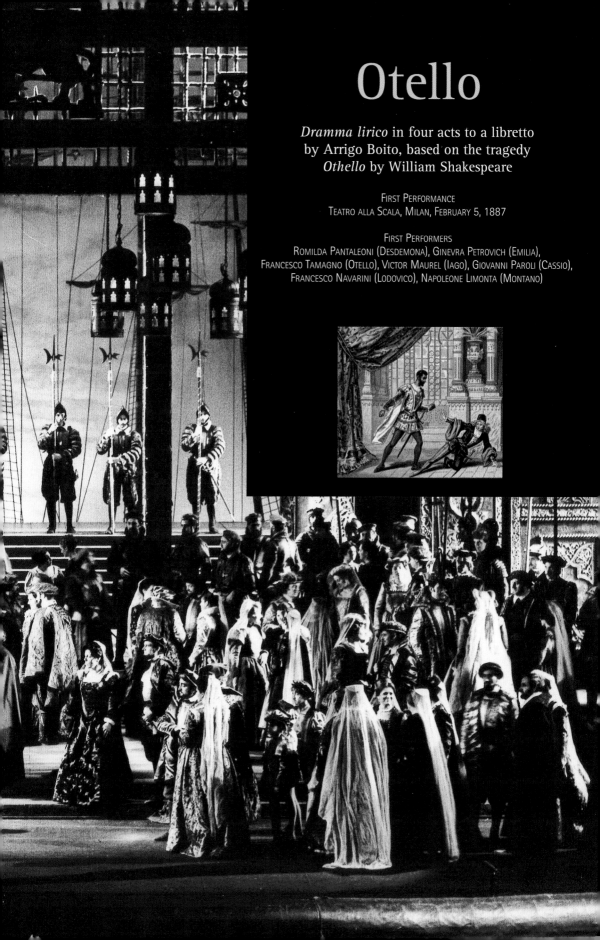

Otello

Dramma lirico in four acts to a libretto
by Arrigo Boito, based on the tragedy
Othello by William Shakespeare

FIRST PERFORMANCE
TEATRO ALLA SCALA, MILAN, FEBRUARY 5, 1887

FIRST PERFORMERS
ROMILDA PANTALEONI (DESDEMONA), GINEVRA PETROVICH (EMILIA),
FRANCESCO TAMAGNO (OTELLO), VICTOR MAUREL (IAGO), GIOVANNI PAROLI (CASSIO),
FRANCESCO NAVARINI (LODOVICO), NAPOLEONE LIMONTA (MONTANO)

CHARACTERS

Otello, a Moor, general of the Venetian army (*tenor*)
Iago, an ensign (*baritone*)
Cassio, a captain (*tenor*)
Roderigo, a Venetian gentleman (*tenor*)
Lodovico, an ambassador of the Venetian republic (*bass*)
Montano, Otello's predecessor as governor of Cyprus (*bass*)
Desdemona, Otello's wife (*soprano*)
Emilia, Iago's wife (*mezzo-soprano*)
A herald (*bass*)

CHORUSES AND EXTRAS
Soldiers and sailors of the Venetian republic; Venetian gentlewomen and gentlemen; Cypriot people of both sexes; Greek, Dalmatian, and Albanian men-at-arms; island children; an innkeeper; four servants at the inn; ordinary sailors

TIME: The end of the 15th century.
PLACE: A coastal city on the island of Cyprus.

Above: The concertato in Act III of *Otello* in the famous 1976 La Scala production. Conducted by Carlos Kleiber; direction, sets, and costumes by Franco Zeffirelli.

PLOT

Act I

Outside the castle, Otello's home, facing a port. It is evening, a violent storm rages, and a crowd of people on the shore watch, powerless, as Otello's ship struggles to reach the port. The ship finally enters the bay, and Otello appears, announcing the defeat of the Turkish fleet. He then sets off for the castle, where Desdemona awaits him. The onlookers exult in the victory. Roderigo, a Venetian gentleman, confesses to Iago that he is secretly in love with Desdemona. Iago tells him to not lose hope and promises his help; he in turn confesses he hates Otello for promoting Cassio instead of Iago to the rank of captain. He further insinuates to Roderigo that Cassio too desires Desdemona's graces, and then he invites Cassio, who has meanwhile arrived, to drink. Trying to get Cassio drunk, Iago provokes him into a fight with Roderigo, so that in the end the two challenge each other to a duel. Only Otello's intervention restores calm. Furious about what has happened, Otello demotes Cassio and orders Iago to restore calm in the city. When everyone else has left, Otello is finally alone with Desdemona. The two lovers remember the first

moments of their love, and they tenderly embrace and return toward the castle.

Act II

A room off the castle garden. Iago continues to weave his plot: Cassio arrives, upset about the loss of his rank, and Iago suggests that with help from Desdemona he could regain Otello's good graces. Cassio accepts this advice and joins Desdemona in the park.

Iago sees his plot taking shape and approaches Otello, who is watching Cassio and Desdemona, and insinuates to him the suspicion of a secret tie between the two. The Moor drives off any thought of infidelity by Desdemona, but when she asks him to pardon Cassio, he feels the first pangs of jealousy. He violently drives away Desdemona and throws to the ground the handkerchief with which she tried to cool his forehead, damp with perspiration. Emilia picks it up, but before she and Desdemona leave the room Iago manages to take it from her hand. It will be the handkerchief to deliver the final blow to Otello's reason. Iago tells Otello he saw a handkerchief of Desdemona's in the hands of Cassio; he adds that he heard Cassio speak in his

Above: Playbill for the premiere of *Otello*. Teatro alla Scala, Milan, February 5, 1887.

Left: Tenor Plácido Domingo and soprano Mirella Freni, acclaimed interpreters of Otello and Desdemona at La Scala in 1976. This production, which began the 1976–77 season, had particular resonance thanks to La Scala's first-ever live television broadcast of an entire performance.

sleep of his love for Desdemona. Otello swears to get revenge.

Act III

The great hall of the castle. Iago, who has meanwhile hidden Desdemona's handkerchief in Cassio's home, promises Otello that he can get the youth to confess his love. Desdemona again asks

The baritone Victor Maurel (left, as Iago) and the tenor Francesco Tamagno (right, as Otello), splendid and highly esteemed performers in the premiere of the opera at La Scala, on February 5, 1887.

Otello to consider Cassio's plight. Otello does not listen and, with the excuse of a headache, asks her to wrap his forehead with the handkerchief he gave her. Desdemona responds that she doesn't have it. Otello's reaction is violent and unexpected: he accuses Desdemona and hurls at her the most atrocious insults, making her flee in tears. Left alone, Otello thinks of Desdemona's guilt. Iago arrives with Cassio, and Otello hides behind a column. Iago gets Cassio to talk about Bianca, his lover. Cassio smiles and shows Iago a handkerchief that he has found in his room.

The distressed Otello can hear only the laughter and fragments of the conversation and believes the two are talking about Desdemona. Trumpet blasts announce the arrival of Lodovico, the Venetian ambassador, and Cassio leaves.

The ambassador bears a message from the doge, which Otello reads to those present: he has been recalled to Venice, and Cassio is proclaimed his successor in the rule of Cyprus. While reading the document, Otello watches Desdemona to see her reactions, and amid general amazement he hurls himself at her and throws her to the floor. All those present then leave, and as though crazed, Otello is left incoherent and faints. Iago looks at him on the floor and salutes him ironically as "the Lion of Venice."

Act IV

Desdemona's bedchamber. It is night, and with her soul burdened by sad thoughts, she sends away Emilia and awaits Otello. She prays and then lies down. Otello appears and contemplates the sleeping Desdemona for a long moment before leaning over her and kissing her. At this she awakens. In severe tones he tells her to recommend herself to God because he has come to kill her. She tries desperately to defend herself and proclaims herself innocent, but Otello grabs her by the throat and strangles her. Emilia knocks at the door. Otello lets her enter and she declares that Cassio has killed Roderigo. Desdemona's weak voice can be heard. Emilia hears her last breath and then flees, calling for help. Lodovico, Cassio, and Iago enter. In a short time Iago's terrible plot is revealed, as is confirmed also by the arrival of Montano: Roderigo, before dying, accused Iago. He flees, followed by the guards. Otello draws his dagger and stabs himself; he then drags himself to Desdemona's bed and, dying, kisses her for the last time.

BACKGROUND AND ANALYSIS

Sixteen years of silence separate *Otello* from *Aida*, a long period interrupted only by the *Messa da Requiem* (1874) and the revision of *Simon Boccanegra* (1884). The interlude was indeed long, but by no means does that mean Verdi was somehow in the shadows. Whether intentionally or not, he found himself at the center of controversies as well as romantic scandals. To make sense of this we must follow the proper order.

In 1872, after the Milan premiere of *Aida*, Verdi had to refute the charge that he was an "imitator of Wagner." As he wrote to Ricordi: "Fine result, after 35 years of a career to end up an imitator!!!" He was at the center of a battle related to a skilled propaganda campaign orchestrated by the Casa Editrice Lucca, Wagner's publisher in Italy, against the hegemony of the Casa Ricordi. The controversy divided public and critics alike and eventually created two camps: Verdians and Wagnerians. The latter were the fruit of a snobbish culture, quick to accuse the former of being tied to a "popular" composer.

There were enormous differences between the two composers, and without going into detail it should be enough to analyze the ways in which they addressed the theater. On one side was Verdi, who never lost sight of the public, which he believed had to be touched, moved to the point of tears. On the other was Wagner, who with his *Zukunftsmusik* ("music of the future") created a kind of contempt for the public that, by way of the avant-garde, has endured to our day. Thus even today one can discern a certain aloofness in Wagner devotees with regard to the works of Verdi.

For his part, Verdi attended the Italian premiere of *Lohengrin* at Bologna's Teatro Comunale in November 1871 and remained attentive to the German composer's later works, but he was always prudent and made no official statements on Wagner's music. In private, however, he let loose with defensive polemics. In fact, after the Turin performances of *Die Walküre* and *Die Meistersinger von Nürnberg*, he wrote,

A famous drawing from a special issue of the periodical *L'Illustrazione Italiana* dedicated to Verdi's *Otello*.

"This music is fine in the German setting; in ours, no. But in Germany, it goes and goes. As soon as the curtain rises, poof! The lights go out and we're in the dark like quail. In that darkness, in that dead air, we remain numb. . . . But even the Germans nod off!"

When Wagner died, in February of 1883, a deeply shocked Verdi wrote, "Sad. Wagner is dead! Reading the dispatches yesterday I will say I was aghast! Let's not talk about it. It is a great individuality that has vanished! A name that will leave a powerful impression on the history of art!"

Let us leave Wagner. On August 22, 1875, the *Rivista Indipendente*, a Florentine scandal sheet, announced revelations of "certain intimacies of Signora Stolz with Maestro [Angelo] Mariani, and now with Maestro Verdi." On this subject the truth has never been established. Verdi and Strepponi did go through a difficult time between 1872 and 1875, as is clear from her letters of that period. Certainly Teresa Stolz, a frequent visitor to the Verdi home, was a woman of enormous fascination and one of the singers Verdi most admired. As for Verdi and Mariani, who died in 1873, they were in a crisis for about two years. The correspondence of Stolz and of Mariani with Verdi reveals nothing. However things actually went, beginning in 1875 the relationship of Verdi and Strepponi was clearly improving. On September 8, 1878, her sixty-third birthday, she gave Verdi a portrait of herself with the dedication "To my Verdi, with the affection and veneration of the past! Peppina!"

Verdi's life followed normal rhythms. He dedicated himself to his farm; he even went hunting briefly, but he soon repented and became a firm defender of animal rights, even prohibiting hunting on his property. He spent the winter in Genoa, occasionally going to Milan to visit friends and to Montecatini to "take the waters" at the spa, all without a thought of composing. Giulio Ricordi and the orchestra director Franco Faccio, with Strepponi's complicity, besieged him. The three managed to get Verdi to meet with Arrigo Boito; Verdi harbored a certain mistrust for Boito, who, like Faccio, was considered a "warm admirer of Wagner." The next move was up to Ricordi, who convinced Verdi to revise *Simon Boccanegra*, naturally with Boito's assistance.

The new *Simon Boccanegra* opened in 1881, after which discussions resumed on what Verdi, Boito, and Ricordi referred to as "a chocolate project." The gestation for *Otello* was long, perhaps Verdi's longest. Boito already had the libretto ready, but Verdi of course was not one to accept things without due consideration. Not at all intimidated, he made his usual requests for changes. The true composition began in 1884. In October of 1885 Verdi started the instrumentation. On November 1, 1886, Boito received a note from Verdi that read, "Dear Boito, it's finished! Good health to us (and also to Him!!!). Farewell. G. Verdi."

Amid great expectation, *Otello* premiered on February 5, 1887. It was a triumph! Verdi commented, "This stir over an opera, all this praise and adulation, make me think of the past (we know how the old always praise their own times), when we, almost without knowing anyone, presented our work to the public, and if they applauded we said, or did not say, 'Thanks,' and if they whistled, 'See you again next time.' I don't know if that was better, but it was certainly more dignified."

The dramatic intensity of Otello as performed by the tenor Plácido Domingo, Teatro alla Scala, Milan, 1976. Beginning with this La Scala production, the Spanish singer became the most complete and acclaimed modern performer of the role.

One notes immediately the definitive transcending of opera as a series of set pieces, and again one speaks of "Wagnerian influence." Dramatic unity was always one aim of Verdi's theatrical art, and this is clear in the complexity of the vocal language, a composite recitative-arioso style that often approaches speech. Certainly *Otello* displays an "experimental" language. The detachment from the world of melody is obvious; the melodic phrases in *Otello* are so large they are nearly impossible to fix in the memory. Except for Desdemona's "Willow Song," everything proceeds in fragments, short sections of tunes that are certainly not random but indissolubly tied to the characters.

The structure of the opera is far simpler and more clearly defined than the Shakespearean tragedy. With his characteristic lucidity and talent for synthesis, Verdi focused his attention on the three main characters. Iago is outstanding, drawn by Verdi not only as an incarnation of evil but also as a person "indifferent to everything, unbelieving,

lively." His singing swings from *mezza voce* ("half voice") passages, in which he "becomes more terrible," to moments of dramatic emphasis and exuberance, such as in the "Credo" ("I believe") or in the duet "Sì, per il ciel marmoreo giuro!" ("Yes, by the marble heavens I swear!").

Otello is no less complex, even if he might seem more naïve, a slave to a primitive, jealous instinct. The way Verdi draws his character is fascinating: the more he falls into the abyss of jealousy, the more his melodic language crumbles, as in "Fuggirmi io sol non so!" ("I alone cannot flee myself!") at the end of Act III. His attempts to escape the poison of jealousy are tied to efforts at memory, to the search for his glorious past: "Ora e per sempre addio, sante memorie" ("Now and forever farewell, holy memories").

Generally dismissed as colorless, Desdemona is rather a memorable character with the dreamy femininity of a woman in love, and in the name of that feeling she assumes, in Act IV, a sublime, sacrificial greatness, a musical body, as she prepares for death.

Above, top: "The Willow Song," in Act IV of *Otello*, performed here by the soprano Katia Ricciarelli, Teatro La Fenice, Venice, 1979.

Above: The soprano Mirella Freni, an interpreter of "historic" stature in the role of Desdemona, Teatro alla Scala, Milan, 1976.

[...] The harmonies of the introduction sink from the chromatic violence in C major (for 250 beats the organ holds on its pedals three notes, C–C-sharp–D, purposefully "dirty") to a diatonic dissolve into E major, which accompanies the calming of the storm. In the preparation for the duet, small chromatic oscillations foretell the treatment of the vocal lines of Otello and Desdemona, rendered uncertain sometimes by the sudden wrinkling of the melody into small intervals, at other times by impetuous outbursts with an affirmative character that drown in unstable harmonies, in the delays of the fifth and the linking of minor and major ninths, and in the difficult tonal resolutions, which give a feeling of stickiness unusual for a form traditionally used to convey positive accents.

The choral timbres are primarily homophonic, not without the occasional breaking of lines between different sections, with triumphal ("Vittoria"–"Victory") or descriptive significance aided by Boito's precious wording "splende, s'oscura, palpita, oscilla" ("It shines, hides, pulses, swings") during the celebration.

The instrument as symbol characterizes the treatment of the orchestra, so that the piccolo rises above the others during the storm; the cellos, violins, and violas accompany, alternately, Otello and Desdemona in the dark tonality of G-flat major dear to 19th-century melodramatic pathos; the English horn, clarinets, and bass clarinet follow the ascending route of the duet, from the low registers of the cellos to higher tones and harmonies, up to the final hovering of the voices and the violin trill.

In Acts II and III the musical "color" of the characters prevails over the structure; the recitative, with continual passages of climax, forms the connective tissue of the two acts, but at some moments it arrives at abbreviations of closed forms that throw sudden light on the characters and dramatic situations. The "Credo" of Iago, for example, is the second part of a "scherzo," a kind of trio, whose dancing tone takes on sinister colorations announced by the "motto" later repeated by Puccini at the beginning of *Turandot*. Very complex is the placement of one conventionally developed scene: the chorus and quartet of Desdemona, Emilia, Otello, and Iago. The auroral entrance of the cho-

rus in E major (the key previously used to mark the end of the storm) suspends the scene between Otello and Iago on the empty fourths (B–E) of Iago's warning ("Vigilate"–"Be vigilant"). The resumption of the scene gives the chorus and quartet the sense of a lyric parenthesis, framing them like relics of bygone conventions, and as such used to represent an environment extraneous to the dramatic debate between Otello and Iago, with the result that the official serenity of Desdemona's procession and her innocence as Otello's wife do not, for the moment, have any points of contact. The duet of the tenor and the baritone ("Sì, pel ciel"–"Yes, by heaven") that concludes the act is likewise detritus from melodramatic conventions, and it has the same feeling as the male duet in *I Puritani*, marking the conclusion of a pact; but in *Otello* the pact is baleful, and the positive sense of the duet is alienated, undergoing a mutation in the negative sense.

Portrait of the writer, composer, and librettist Arrigo Boito. A leading member of the Scapigliatura movement in Milan, and a musician himself, he made the ideal collaborator for Verdi.

Act II has other estranging effects created by symbolic references to conventional closed forms. Such is the case in Act with Otello's "Esultate" ("Rejoice") and Iago's "Se un fragil voto di femmina" ("If a woman's frail vow"), both ghosts of the traditional entrance aria that offer symbols of it in the high heroic tenor and the baritonal comic touches, but these touches contrast with the dramatic situation to create sinister effects, the very ones needed for the image of Iago. Act II's "Ora e per sempre addio" ("Farewell, now and forever") retains the motions of the cabaletta, with its martial tones and rhythms, but these are negated by the sense the piece assumes within the drama. A similar schism between form and meaning is evident in "Era la notte" ("It was night"), which is as suited to Iago's perfidy as its pastoral *siciliana* formulation in C major is not. Verdi's syncopation, so often used for tumultuous moments—recognitions, encounters, escapes—assumes an anguished tone when it loses its typical motor to depict, in a refreshing subversion of the formula, Otello's doubt: Credo leale Desdemona, e credo che non o sia" ("I believe Desdemona is loyal, and I believe she is not").

Even in Act III, the official thematic repetitions that frame the scene in which Otello's threats set off Desdemona's typi-

offers an inversion of conventional values, between the scene, dominated by the steadiness of the vocal line over the instrumental theme (Otello's A-flat–E-flat recalling the B–E of Iago's "Vigilate"), and the aria, a much less effective lyric parenthesis, burdened by the static feeling of the traditional closed form. In the scene between Iago and Cassio, the song "Questa è una ragna" ("This is a web") is a grotesque reflection of the French-style aria with its *éclat de rire* (roar of laughter), also used in "È scherzo od è follia" from *Un Ballo in Maschera*. The end of the act is a compromise between the regularity of the finale, beginning with Desdemona's largo "A terra!" ("Down!"), and the insertion of a coda with Otello's fainting and Iago's triumph, in which Verdi adapted his need to write a theatrical "piece" to his desire for a less conventional conclusion, also supported by Boito, forever gutting the usual act finale, which is set in motion and then negated in the span of only a few beats.

In Act IV the modal harmonization of the "Willow Song" and the prayer, in which Gabriele Baldini sees the legacy of feminine prayers going back to *I Lombardi*, creates an atmosphere already known to Violetta, that of a nocturne within four walls, and violently contrasts with the return of the recitative animated by the restless sixteenth-note motive that

The note written by Verdi after finishing the score of *Otello*: "Dear Boito, it's finished! Good health to us (and also to Him!!!). Farewell. G. Verdi."

Falstaff

Commedia lirica in three acts to a libretto by
Arrigo Boito, based on William Shakespeare's
comedy *The Merry Wives of Windsor* and
passages from *Henry IV*

FIRST PERFORMANCE
TEATRO ALLA SCALA, MILAN, FEBRUARY 9, 1893

FIRST PERFORMERS
EMMA ZILLI (ALICE), ADELINA STEHLE (NANNETTA), VIRGINIA GUERRINI (MEG),
GIUSEPPINA PASQUA (QUICKLY), EDOARDO GARBIN (FENTON),
VICTOR MAUREL (FALSTAFF), ANTONIO PINI-CORSI (FORD),
GIOVANNI PAROLI (DR. CAIUS), PAOLO PELAGALLI-ROSSETTI (BARDOLFO),
VITTORIO ARIMONDI (PISTOLA)

CHARACTERS

Sir John Falstaff (*baritone*)
Fenton (*tenor*)
Dr. Caius (*tenor*)
Bardolfo (Bardolph),
follower of Falstaff (*tenor*)
Pistola (Pistol), follower
of Falstaff (*bass*)
Mrs. Alice Ford (*soprano*)
Ford, Alice's husband
(*baritone*)
Nannetta, their daughter
(*soprano*)
Mistress Quickly (*mezzo-soprano*)
Mrs. Meg Page (*mezzo-soprano*)
Mine Host at the Garter
(*silent*)
Robin, Falstaff's page
(*silent*)
Ford's page (*silent*)

CHORUSES AND EXTRAS
Burghers and populace;
Ford's servants; masked
people dressed as elves,
fairies, witches, etc.

TIME: During the reign
of England's Henry IV.
PLACE: England, in Windsor.

Below: Poster for the premiere performance of *Falstaff*, Teatro alla Scala, Milan, February 9, 1893.

PLOT

Act I

The Garter Inn. Sir John Falstaff, an elderly knight with unrealistic amorous ambitions not yet satisfied, has just written two identical letters, addressed to two beautiful gentlewomen of Windsor, Alice Ford and Meg Page, who he believes are in love with him. The old knight has rudely dispatched Dr. Caius, who accused Falstaff's two underlings, Bardolfo and Pistola, of robbery. Falstaff orders Bardolfo and Pistola to deliver his letters, but they refuse, as it would be beneath their honor. Falstaff immediately calls a page and sends him off with the letters. Then, after philosophizing on the meaning of honor, he snatches up a broom and drives them out of the inn.

Garden outside the Ford home. Alice and Meg realize that Falstaff has sent them both identical declarations of love. They are greatly amused and decide to teach him a good lesson. Their friend Mistress Quickly will pretend to be a kindly go-between and will invite Falstaff to Alice's home.

In turn, Bardolfo and Pistola have gone to Ford and revealed to him Falstaff's intentions. The jealous Ford, with the help of the offended Dr. Caius, is also ready to punish Falstaff. He plans to visit Falstaff under a false name and provoke him into revealing the truth.

Act II

The Garter Inn. While Falstaff drinks, Bardolfo and Pistola enter, ask to rejoin his service, and announce the visit of a

his advances go too far, Meg and Quickly burst in; Ford is about to arrive, furiously searching for his wife and her lover. Falstaff hides behind a screen, from which he watches as Ford, followed by Fenton, Caius, Bardolfo, Pistola, and other men turn everything upside down in their search. As soon as Ford moves on to another room, the women hide Falstaff in a laundry basket. Now the screen offers shelter to the young Fenton and Nannetta, who in that bustle find the time to flirt. Their effusions mislead Ford, convinced that the screen hides Falstaff with Alice.

Above: The baritone Mariano Stabile, one of the leading interpreters of the role of Falstaff, in 1958.

Left: An issue of *L'Illustrazione Italiana* dedicated to the world premiere of *Falstaff*.

Opposite: The Garter Inn in Act I of the opera. The baritone Renato Bruson is Falstaff, the tenor Alessandro Cosentino is Bardolfo, and the bass Luigi Rona is Pistola. Teatro Regio, Parma, 1994.

woman. This is Quickly, who with a ceremonious and adulatory air confides in Falstaff that Alice Ford awaits him at her home in the early afternoon.

Falstaff, gloatingly in seventh heaven, now receives yet a second visit; this is "Signor Fontana" (the disguised Ford). Without too much of an introduction he proposes a deal: with his irresistible charm, Falstaff should conquer the bashful Alice Ford for himself and then later pass her on to Fontana. The knight assures him the undertaking will go off with complete success.

A room in the Ford home. The conniving women have prepared the scene, missing only the principal actor. Falstaff arrives, full of confidence, and Alice feigns timidity and reluctance in the face of the knight's assaults. Before

When the fragile obstacle is knocked aside, the two youths are surprised. Ford chases Fenton while Alice orders four servants to empty the laundry basket (with Falstaff) into the Thames below. She points out the scene to her husband, and everyone bursts into riotous laughter.

Act III
The Garter Inn. Sunset. Falstaff, numb from the cold and humiliated, meditates bitterly on the situation of his life.

While he finds comfort in a glass of warm wine, the obsequious Quickly approaches and again manages to flatter the ingenuous knight into a new tryst, this one at midnight in the Royal Park, where he must go dressed as the Black Huntsman, with a black cloak and two long deer antlers on his head. Falstaff goes off with Quickly while Alice, Ford, and the others meet in the park, dressed as spirits, elves, and witches. Ford, however, holds back with Caius and promises him that while everyone is

knight. As the twelve bells of midnight toll, Falstaff emerges from the darkness. He feels a little ridiculous and grotesque in that strange costume, but as soon as he spots Alice he launches into a new, passionate courtship.

This idyll is brief. The frightened voice of Meg announces the arrival of the fairies, and soon the scene is completely invaded by woodland spirits, devils, nymphs, and elves that rush toward Falstaff, mocking him and beating him up. In the heat of the fake assem-

The great Herne's Oak in Act III of *Falstaff* in the 1994 production at the Teatro Regio, Parma. Conducted by Gustav Kuhn, directed by Mario Corradi, sets by Koki Fregni, costumes by Nica Magnani.

masked he will take the opportunity to set up Caius's wedding to Nannetta that very night. From a hiding place behind a tree, Quickly overhears all of this and vows to foil their plan.

Herne's Oak in the Royal Park. Fenton intones a love sonnet to Nannetta, who appears masked as the queen of the fairies, followed by Alice and the other wives, ready to welcome the

bly of spirits, the knight recognizes Bardolfo and understands that he is being made a fool of. He is not the only one, however: Ford, who had organized the betrothal of his daughter to Caius, is fooled by the costumes and thus tricked into giving his consent to the marriage of Nannetta and Fenton. Everyone laughs happily, while Ford realizes his only choice is to pardon them for the hoax.

BACKGROUND AND ANALYSIS

In 1887, with the clamor of *Otello* behind him, Verdi returned to the daily routine of country life at Sant'Agata, along with various charitable activities, including the construction of a hospital at Villanova near Sant'Agata and, using the money he'd made on *Otello*, buying land in Milan for a retirement home for opera singers. These activities seem to indicate that he had once again set aside his career as a composer, but during one of Arrigo Boito's frequent visits, Verdi provided a quite emblematic explanation: "And now that you have carried off *Otello* and that the public has made it their own, what is left for my long days at Sant'Agata? To live all alone with the fruit of my work was once a reason for great delight; but now that work is no longer mine . . . and I wouldn't have the strength to start again from the beginning." The phrase might seem ambiguous, but Boito, using diplomacy and patience, helped Verdi overcome his doubt and uncertainties by responding, "There is only one way to finish better than with *Otello* and that is to finish victoriously with *Falstaff*. After having sounded all the cries and groans of the human heart, to finish with a mighty burst of laughter! That will astonish!"

This was in July 1889. Verdi overcame his last concerns and responded to Boito: "Amen; and let it be! So let's do *Falstaff*." Boito, perhaps to ward off any future reconsiderations on the part of Verdi, worked rapidly. And Verdi was satisfied: "Dear Boito, Benissimo, benissimo! Before reading your draft I wanted to read *The Merry Wives of Windsor* and the two parts of *Henry IV* and *Henry V*, and I can only repeat, benissimo."

Boito wrote the libretto and delivered it to Verdi in March of 1890: for the

first time Verdi accepted a libretto without making changes and immediately began to set it to music. Over the same month he composed Act I, but then came news of the death of Emanuele Muzio, "a true, devoted friend of nearly fifty years," throwing Verdi into the most profound dejection, "and so I have very little will to write an opera that I began but did not get far with." The composition was not easy; 1891 went by, and it was September of 1892 when Verdi finally gave Ricordi the score, on which he added an aside: "All finished! Go, go, old John . . . go on your way as far as you can. . . . Go, go. Farewell!!!" He knew this was his final opera, his leave-taking from music and the world.

Early in January of 1893 Verdi and Giuseppina moved to Milan. By then in his eighties, Verdi attended the rehearsals with incredible energy and lucidity. The entire world of music had

Above: Adolfo Hohenstein's costume sketch of Quickly and Falstaff for the premiere of *Falstaff*, Act II, Teatro alla Scala, Milan, February 9, 1893.

Opposite (bottom) and below: Two more costume designs by Adolfo Hohenstein for the premiere of *Falstaff*.

Above: The first scene in Act III of *Falstaff*, Teatro Regio, Parma, 1994.

Below: The baritone Juan Pons in the title role in the La Scala production of the 1980–81 season. Conducted by Lorin Maazel, directed by Giorgio Strehler, sets and costumes by Ezio Frigerio.

its eyes on La Scala the evening of February 9, 1893, to triumphantly welcome the last opera by Verdi.

Boito had prepared a perfect theatrical structure on which Verdi constructed an architecture of sounds and singing vivid in its colors, agile in its progression, free in its form and style. In this playful, almost frenetic—but also subtly melancholy—stage machine, Verdi set aside sweetly sentimental lyrical oases for the two young lovers, Fenton and Nannetta. The orchestra was, more than ever, varied and attentive to each detail, to a rhythm more articulated and animated and to a more nuanced sensibility of timbre. Also in the voices Verdi seems to want a sort of "orchestration," pushing the voices to adopt extremely disparate colors and techniques, such as falsetto.

After Milan, Verdi still had the energy to attend the premiere of *Falstaff* in Rome. Then came the time, finally, for rest, but with Verdi this most certainly did not mean inactivity. He wrote ballets for the Parisian performances of *Otello*, followed the construction of the rest home for musicians, and composed the *Te Deum* and the *Stabat Mater*.

Nor did he fail to pay attention to what was going on around him, including the birth of the *giovane scuola* ("young school") of opera. Pietro Mascagni had asserted himself with *Cavalleria Rusticana* (1890), and Ruggero Leoncavallo triumphed with *I Pagliacci* (1892). And yet another composer was making his mark: Giacomo Puccini, who had already composed *Le Villi* (1884), *Edgar* (1889), and *Manon Lescaut* (1893). Verdi noted, "I've heard many good things about the composer Puccini. I've seen a letter that speaks very well of him. He follows modern techniques, and that's natural, but he remains committed to melody, which is neither ancient nor modern. It seems, though, that in his music the symphonic element is dominant! There's nothing wrong with that. But one has to be careful with it. Opera is opera, and symphony is symphony."

In the autumn of 1898, on November 14, following complications with her lungs, Giuseppina died. The singer's will ended with these words: "Now, farewell, my Verdi. As we were united in life, may God rejoin our souls in Heaven." Verdi remained by her side to the last moment.

For Verdi this was a terrible blow. Nearby he had his adopted daughter Maria Carrara-Verdi (his aunt's granddaughter, taken into his home when she was orphaned at age seven) and his faithful friends Arrigo Boito, Teresa Stolz, and Giulio Ricordi. After Giuseppina's death Verdi increasingly distanced himself the hotel, and the street was covered with straw to muffle the sounds of traffic. At 3:10 on January 27, 1901, the 87-year-old Verdi took his last breath. Boito was with him: "The voluntary servitude I dedicated to that just man, so noble and truly great, was the act of my life that satisfied me most."

from Sant'Agata; perhaps being alone in that country house was simply too difficult. By then he spent much of his time in Milan, in a suite in the Hotel Milan on Via Manzoni. He spent Christmas of 1900 with his adopted daughter Maria and his usual friends.

Early in January he wrote to a friend, "As for health, even though the doctors tell me I am not ill, I feel that everything tires me . . . I'm not living, I'm vegetating . . . what more do I have to do in this world?"

On January 21, while getting dressed in his Milan apartment, he suddenly felt unwell. He survived a few more days: a silent crowd waited anxiously outside

Two months later Boito wrote to the French music critic Camille Bellaigue: "Verdi is dead; he has taken an enormous quantity of light and vital warmth. We had all basked in the sunshine of his Olympian old age. He died magnificently, like a formidable, silent fighter. My dear friend, in my life I have lost those whom I have idolized, and my grief outlived my resignation. But never have I been so surprised by such resentment against death and contempt for this mysterious, blind, stupid, triumphant, and cowardly power. It took the death of this nonagenarian to arouse those feelings. . . . Now all is finished. He sleeps like a king of Spain in the Escorial."

Renato Bruson in the role of Falstaff at the Teatro Regio in Parma, 1994. The baritone also recorded the opera in 1982, under conductor Carlo Maria Giulini.

Nannetta, drawing by Adolfo Hohenstein for the premiere of *Falstaff*, Teatro alla Scala, Milan, February 9, 1893.

today, but what aroused the most admiration of contemporaries was the fact that *Falstaff* had been composed by a man who was seventy-six when he began work and seventy-nine when he finished. Everyone was resoundingly amazed—even scientist believers in positivism, meaning people by definition difficult to amaze, since in their philosophy every event fit into an established plan. In fact, in January of 1893, when Verdi was busy with the rehearsals, Cesare Lombroso, a well-known anthropologist and positivist, wrote an article entitled "The Psychological Phenomenon of Verdi," which ended with these words: "It is more honest to confess that explanations are not to be found, that the anomaly is so great, so extraordinary, as to confound even those who make a special study of this area." So the "miracle" did not seem to be so much the existence of *Falstaff* as the fact that it had been composed at a certain age, almost as if *The Marriage of Figaro* ceased to be miraculous for having been written by a man of thirty, or *The Barber of Seville* for having been written at twenty-three.

The problem is that this strange opinion translated (and, for a few, still translates) into a great misunderstanding concerning the nature of this opera, which has typically been described as youthful, overflowing with youthfulness. So Verdi, a sane and "normal" man par excellence, was revealed to be instead some sort of monster. In reality, *Falstaff* is a typically "senile" work, namely an expression of the mind of a man who, at the end of a long and highly industrious life, turns back to contemplate that life with melancholy, but also serene, detachment. Everything in *Falstaff* has softened outlines as in an operation of mature memory; all is smoothed as if seen through a veil. At the time of *Otello* Verdi

as an equal, on the same plane, in *Falstaff* the loves of Fenton and Nannetta are seen with the tender eyes of a grandfather, the hoax of masquerade fades into a romantic reverie, and all the rest comes in only through the filter of irony. This is the specific poetry of *Falstaff*: the fact that its author shows his years, all of them.

To the overwhelming majority of critics, and from every country, *Falstaff* is Verdi's most perfect opera, the one that combines all his virtues while wiping away every trace of dross, lifting his virtues to a higher plane. It is, all told, his masterpiece. Here Verdi brings to complete maturation his transcending of those "closed forms" that from Wagner on had been judged by many to belong to an inferior phase of music drama. This transcendence was already visible in *Otello* (in which the structural unit was the scene, not the aria), but not in such a radical way, for in *Falstaff* only vestiges of strophic forms remain. In relation to this trascendence, the orchestral writing is more agile and mobile, purged of such stereotypical procedures as repeated chords, and animated by a more varied sense of harmony, one more sensitive to detail. Because of these virtues, *Falstaff* (together with *Otello* and the *Messa da Requiem*, but with greater efficacy) reconciled to Verdi all or most of those who (in Italy but most of all elsewhere) had until then considered him a composer who was more or less brilliant but rough and uneven.

Those in opposition to this opinion, meaning those who continued to assert the superiority of the Verdi of *La Traviata*, *Il Trovatore*, *Un Ballo in Maschera*, or *Aida* over the Verdi of *Falstaff*, were and are few among modernist musicians and even fewer among scholars and critics. In the first group it will suffice to mention Stravinsky; the second group includes Eduard Hanslick and, in Italy, Bruno Barilli and S. A. Luciani, along with Gabriele Baldini and the author of this text.

However, in art, questions of precedence and rank always hide a second sense, which of course is the important one. To the extent that it is possible to determine such things, it is not overly important to know if *Aida* is worth more or less than *Falstaff*. Nor is it important to ascertain whether the ungrammatical verses by Francesco Maria Piave are truly worse than the erudite, bizarre ones by Arrigo Boito. What is important is to understand how the change in subjects and in forms that passed between the Verdi up until *Aida* and the Verdi of later works cannot be reduced to explanations of a "personal evolution," the mysterious caprices of which are a result of the most glorious genius of Giuseppe Verdi, who, having passed the age of seventy, felt the need to conform with the rules of good taste then reigning in "European" music. Without doubt, a personal evolution did take place in Verdi, but it was strongly affected by the general historical situation. He was the cantor who sang the people's soul of the Risorgimento—which was based on the sentimental and moral categories of an eminently popular mythology that demanded certain forms and certain styles (perhaps also—why not?—verses such as those by Piave) that were roughly the opposite of that day's "European" music—and so he remained as long as that soul appeared open to the formation of a new national awareness. But things slowly changed, and in the 1880s the bourgeois solution of the Risorgimento, with Milan as its moral capital, was a *fait accompli*, sanctioned by custom. And as if to be reminded of this, Verdi found himself facing Arrigo Boito, a representative of that cultural pretension that was the essence of the cosmopolitan aspirations of the triumphant class.

And it is well understood that Verdi remained Verdi, a creator with an extraordinary wellspring of energy and bound to his own past. That did not keep him from assimilating the new demands in his own way. The "historical" interest of his two last theatrical masterpieces (and also of the *Pezzi Sacri* [*Sacred Pieces*] that followed) is essentially here, which also presents the problem, until now never confronted, of the clandestine connections between this last Verdi and the French opera of the time—the French opera, a daughter of the middle class that was the mother of all European middle classes, that had so much influence on Puccini and on the other composers of the so-called *giovane scuola*. Those composers, in fact, were not at all influenced by the Verdi from before *Otello*; but some were undoubtedly influenced by the one from after it (just think of how *Falstaff* affected Puccini's *Gianni Schicchi*).

One of the numerous scenes from *Falstaff* used on Liebig trading cards.

Otello and, even more, *Falstaff* are thus the only operas by Verdi that to some degree extend into the new century. It would be better to say they are the only ones that, despite their roots lying deep in Italian tradition, have more than a passing relationship with the European musical culture of their time—at least in the ideals they present, if not always in the ways in which they put those ideals into practice. Both of them, but most of all *Falstaff*, have a hint of ambiguity that only the supreme mastery of their realization manages to overshadow, but that in the end is not the ultimate reason for their fascination. [...]

Fedele D'Amico,
Guida all'Opera,
Arnoldo Mondadori Editore

The publisher sincerely thanks the following for their
invaluable help with the picture research for this book:
Teatro alla Scala, Milan
Fondazione Teatro La Fenice, Venice
Teatro Regio, Parma
Teatro Comunale, Bologna
Teatro Municipale, Piacenza

The author gives special thanks to the following
for their help and collaboration:
Cristiano Chiarot and Barbara Montagner of the
Press Office of La Fenice, Venice
Marina Dorigo of the Historical Archive of La Fenice,
Venice
Ms. Pellegrini of the Historical Archive of the Teatro
Regio, Parma
Lukas Franceschini and Valerio Maggioni

that he or she has undergone peer scrutiny and meets a high set of standards."

Contrary to the television myth, laboratory workers differ from crime scene searchers. Scientists, most with advanced degrees, differ from the technicians who lend them support.

It is the scientists who wield the mighty swords. And, sadly, not all are equally competent. Not all view themselves as champions of scientific truth.

206 Bones is the story of a scientist who wished to become the Grail Knight. Though qualified in one field, the individual aspired to much more. The result was disastrous.

I have selected forensic science as my life work. Like the vast majority of my colleagues, I have sworn to a code of chivalry. The pledge: To protect the innocent from wrongful conviction; to help convict the guilty.

The fulfillment of this twofold promise requires assurance of professional competence across all disciplines, and enforcement of rigorous ethical standards.

How to ensure both?

Tempe and the NAS are right on the mark. Board certification must become mandatory in the hiring of scientists, and in their qualification as experts in court.

And existing boards must not relax their standards to accommodate all. Technicians are not scientists. The skill sets are different. Certification standards must remain rigorous to clarify this distinction.

Not perfect. But it's a start.

What do I propose?

Proclaimed to all knights of the realm. Going forth from this day. To sit at the round table ye must:

Suck it up, take your boards, pass the king's muster.

Déjà Dead

Kathy Reichs

The Number One Bestseller

The bones of a woman are discovered in the grounds of an abandoned monastery. The case is given to Dr Temperance Brennan of the Laboratoire de Medecine Legale in Montreal: 'too decomposed for standard autopsy. Request anthropological expertise. My case. ' Brennan becomes convinced that a serial killer is at work, despite the deep cynicism of Detective Claudel who heads the investigation. Dr. Brennan's forensic expertise and contacts at Quantico finally convince him otherwise, but only after the body count has grown and the lives of those closest to her are more than just endangered.

'Better than Patricia Cornwell'
Express on Sunday

'A guaranteed sleep-deterrent. Genuinely thrilling'
Literary Review

arrow books

ALSO AVAILABLE IN ARROW

Bare Bones

Kathy Reichs

It's one of the hottest summers on record and forensic anthropologist Dr Temperance Brennan is looking forward to a long overdue vacation. But it's not to be . . .

First, the bones of a newborn baby are found in a wood stove; the mother, barely a child herself, has disappeared.

Next, a Cessna flies into a rock face. The bodies of the pilot and passenger are burned beyond recognition, and covered in an unknown substance.

And then a cache of bones is found in a remote corner of the county. But what happened there, and who will the next victim be? The answers lie hidden deep within the bones – if only Tempe can decipher them in time . . .

'The forensic detail is harrowing, the pace relentless, and the prose assured. Kathy Reichs just gets better and better and is now the Alpha female of this genre'
Irish Independent

'Reichs has now proved that she is up there with the best'
The Times

'Better than Patricia Cornwell'
Sunday Express

arrow books

Monday Mourning

Kathy Reichs

Three skeletons are found in the basement of a pizza parlour.

The building is old, with a colourful past, and Homicide Detective Luc Claudel dismisses the remains as historic. Not his case, not his concern . . .

But forensic anthropologist Tempe Brennan has her doubts. Something about the bones of the three young women suggests a different message: murder. A cold case, but Claudel's case nonetheless.

Brennan is in Montreal to testify as an expert witness at a trial. Digging up more bones was not on her agenda. And to make matters worse, her sometime-lover Detective Andrew Ryan disappears just as Tempe is beginning to trust him.

Soon Tempe finds herself drawn ever deeper into a web of evil from which there may be no escape: three women have disappeared, never to return. And Tempe may be next . . .

'Reichs is not just "as good as" Cornwell, she has become the finer writer'
Daily Express

'Terrific'
Independent on Sunday

arrow books

ALSO AVAILABLE IN ARROW

Cross Bones

Kathy Reichs

**An orthodox Jew is found shot dead in Montreal, the
mutilated body is barely recognisable.**

**Extreme heat has accelerated decomposition, and made it
virtually impossible to determine the trajectory of the bullet.**

But just as forensic anthropologist Dr Temperance Brennan is
attempting to make sense of the fracture patterning, a mysterious
stranger slips her a photograph of a skeleton, assuring her it holds
the key to the victim's death . . .

The trail of clues leads all the way to the Holy Land where,
together with detective Andrew Ryan, Tempe makes a startling
discovery – but the further Tempe probes into the identity of the
ancient skeleton, the more she seems to be putting herself in
danger . . .

'Reichs is on top form. Her writing has an extra energy . . . and
a new confidence'
Sunday Times

'A rattling good read' Kate Mosse

arrow books

Break No Bones

Kathy Reichs

A decomposing body is uncovered in a shallow grave off a lonely beach . . .

The skeleton is articulated, the bone fresh and the vertebrae still connected by soft-tissue – it's a recent burial, and a case forensic anthropologist Dr Temperance Brennan must take.

Dental remains and skeletal gender and race indicators suggest that the deceased is a middle-aged white male – but who was he? Why was he buried in a clandestine grave? And what does the unusual fracture of the sixth cervical vertebra signify?

But just as Brennan is trying to piece together the evidence, another body is discovered – and before long Tempe finds herself drawn deeper into a shocking and chilling investigation, set to challenge her entire view of humanity . . .

'A brilliant novel . . . Reichs's seamless blending of fascinating science and dead-on psychological portrayals, not to mention a whirlwind of a plot, make *Break No Bones* a must-read'
Jeffery Deaver

arrow books

ALSO AVAILABLE IN ARROW

Bones to Ashes

Kathy Reichs

Under the microscope, the outer bone surface is a moonscape of craters . . .

The skeleton is that of a young girl, no more than fourteen years old – and forensic anthropologist Dr Temperance Brennan is struggling to keep her emotions in check.

A nagging in her subconscious won't let up. A memory triggered, deep in her hindbrain – the disappearance of a childhood friend; no warning, no explanation . . .

Detective Andrew Ryan is working a series of parallel cases: three missing persons, three unidentified bodies – all female, all early-to-mid teens . . . Could Tempe's skeleton be yet another in this tragic line of young victims? Or is she over-reacting, making connections where none exist?

Working on instinct, Tempe takes matters into her own hands. But even she couldn't have predicted the horrors this investigation would eventually uncover . . . Can Tempe maintain a professional distance as the past catches up with her in this, her most deeply personal case yet?

arrow books

Devil Bones

Kathy Reichs

An underground chamber is exposed in a seedy, dilapidated house with sagging trim and peeling paint . . .

In the dark cellar, a ritualistic display is revealed. A human skull rests on a cauldron, surrounded by slain chickens and bizarre figurines. Beads and antlers dangle overhead.

Called to the scene is forensic anthropologist Dr Temperance Brennan. Bony architecture suggests that the skull is that of a young, black female. But how did she die? And when? Then, just as Tempe is working to determine post-mortem interval, another body is discovered: a headless corpse carved with Satanic symbols.

As citizen vigilantes, blaming Devil-worshippers, begin a witch-hunt, intent on revenge, Tempe struggles to keep her emotions in check. But the truth she eventually uncovers proves more shocking than even she could have imagined . . .

arrow books

ALSO AVAILABLE IN ARROW

Grave Secrets

Kathy Reichs

The Number One Bestseller

Chupan Ya, Guatemala: Dr Temperance Brennan, forensic anthropologist, is working on one of the most heartbreaking cases of her career, searching the remains of mass graves for the bodies of women and children.

As Tempe digs in the cold, damp pit, the soil begins to yield ash and cinders. Its colour changes from mahogany to graveyard black. Her trowel touches something hard. The bone of a child no more than two years old. Something savage happened twenty years ago.

And something savage is happening today. Four girls are missing from Guatemala City, one of them the daughter of the Canadian Ambassador. A skeleton is found in a septic tank at the back of a run-down hotel. Only someone with Tempe's expertise can deduce who the victim was and how they died. But her path is blocked. It appears that some people would prefer that Chupan Ya stayed buried. And others want the missing girls kept the same way . . .

'Tightly written . . . *Grave Secrets* is a serious and chilling book that is several cuts above most crime fiction. Reichs has proved that she is now up there with the best' *The Times*

arrow books